Short Plays
and
Longer Projects

by

Tony Butterfield

**Recommended for mother-tongue, EFL, GCSE
Youth and Amateur Theatre**

Acknowledgements

Grateful thanks are due to Trilokesh Mukherjee, Sue Upton, Jane Tatam, Flemming Nygaard and to Keith Johnstone, for his creative influence over many years

****

Performing Rights (Royalties) do not apply

Photocopying is authorised when five or more books are purchased

Seek authority from: Tony Butterfield "The Firs", Green Lane, Milton-under-Wychwood, Oxon

OX7 6JY

Tel and Fax: 01993 831542

ISBN 0-9545112-0-4

Published by

INTERACT EDUCATIONAL SERVICES

THE PLAYS

"TOMBS" The Pharoah seems to be dying and so there is a quick competition to design his future tomb. Several ideas are submitted – not all practical.

"VISITORS" Aliens from outer space are trying to understand the behaviour of earthmen but misunderstand virtually everything. Even the uses of a football.

"BABY SITTER" A couple are ready for a big night out – with tickets for a favourite opera. But their child behaves strangely when the baby sitters arrive.

"GETTING AHEAD" The latest "transplant" patient is visited by his relatives in hospital. His new head watches on.

"NEWCOMERS" The youth football team is going through a rough patch. Their manager comes up with a unique idea which the team has to respond to.

"THIS IS YOUR LIFE" The contributors are assembled for a rehearsal of "This is Your Life" and taken through their routine. But the subject proves to be elusive.

"WITNESSES" When there is a fatal road accident the police call several witnesses. But all is not quite what it seems.

"-ING" The broadcasters are training future sports reporters.

"INCA THE THINKER" A young Inca returns from his travels, over the Andes. His boss is sceptical of the claims he makes and the news he brings.

"THE MUSEUM" A new-style museum is about to open. The staff meet to explain their involvement but a "guest" from the old school is sceptical. Soon a real crisis hits the project.

"CLOAK DARROW FARM" A group of partisans are in the final stages of planning their major work – to capture an enemy of the state, alive.

"OUT OF THE CUBE" A teenage terrorist is brought to the prison. Several visitors see her but she has to pay the ultimate price.

THE PROJECTS

"SCULPTURES"

"THE VILLAGE"

"CREATING A CHARACTER"

"THE MARTIANS"

"THE BALLOON"

"DEEPEND"

"THE MUSEUM"

"FINDING A JOB"

"INFORMATION BUREAU"

"THE SURGERY"

INTRODUCTION

These PLAYS and PROJECTS have been written for young people and for those who perhaps wish to cut their teeth on presentations of limited scope and length. They are designed in most cases to attract large casts with a whole class or group in mind. The work is evenly shared and could be rehearsed and presented even in the short time scale often available today.

The PLAYS will benefit immensely from a full presentation with direction, parts learnt, costume and props, sound and light where these are available. This is a seminal step from "reading round the class" and will reward those who try it.

Full length plays provide time and space for character and plot development, for sub-plots, exposition and climax. The pieces here employ many characters and a straightforward plot. They do allow for input by the group using them, probably by way of additional improvised activity. Improvisation is vital for young minds and, of course, is closer to life than the delivery of a text. Also young actors are very good at it and often less inhibited than their seniors. It goes without saying that any improvisation must be an extension of the given plot and not some accretion added on, self-indulgently.

The so-called PROJECTS are certainly based on a degree of improvisation. In this respect they can be seen as skeletons for play-making. Most of them stand in the area between drama exercise and short plays. As with all such material they will spawn their own ideas from a lively group. Many texted plays have a resolution, a denouement and are, in a sense, complete. Most of the PROJECTS here have no such completion but leave the actor and the audience with answers to consider. This is no bad thing as much of life seems to follow this complex line with the question proving as important as the answer. These pieces often throw up debate and opinions suitable for developing minds. It would be nice to think that Book 2 in the series could consist of ideas (which have worked!) authored by the young actors. Do let me see them.

These pieces alone or woven together in a mixed bill can involve a large team with work for everyone, however talented. They should give pleasure to a mini-audience.

Of course the PLAYS are not <u>about</u> young people and they are certainly playable by adults. The same applies to the PROJECTS. When used by adults one can introduce an increasing degree of difficulty and subtlety which ensures that they are not "talking down" to their audiences.

'TOMBS'

Casting

Mushtaq   (A Court Official)

Hanif: (His colleague)

C: (First entrants)

D: (First entrants)

E: (Second entrants)

F: (Second entrants)

G: (Third entrants)

H: (Third entrants)

J: (Third entrants)

K: (Fourth entrants)

L: (Fourth entrants)

'TOMBS'

Mushtaq: Morning, Hanif

Hanif: Hello, Mushtaq. How are you?

Mushtaq: Fine. All ready for The Big Day?

Hanif: Yes. It's been a long time coming.

Mushtaq: And the old devil is still alive.

Hanif: Is he? I haven't seen him for some time.

Mushtaq: Where's my file? Here it is - 'Tombs' (*inspects file*) One, two, three, four. It looks as if we've got four coming.

Hanif: They can bring a friend, can't they?

Mushtaq: Yes. It helps them. Let me see if anyone has arrived (*he goes and returns*) Yes, there are some there. We can start. Call in Number – one!

(*First entry – two people*)

Mushtaq: Good morning. Take a seat. I'm Mushtaq, by the way. Chairman of the TOMBS Project. This is my colleague Hanif. (*They greet each other*) Now C & D. We've looked at your idea. Please explain it to us.

C: We think a sphere, a ball shape would be best.

D: Like a football but 100 metres across.

Hanif: So not really like a football?

C: Not really – but the same shape.

Mushtaq: And where does the Pharaoh's body go? Inside?

D: Yes – right in the centre. In a kind of box….

Hanif: Our worry is that the ball may – well, roll into the desert.

D: There C! I warned you about that.

Mushtaq: How about earthquakes and things? How did you plan to build it?

C: We thought of making a small ball of stone and then blowing it up with a bicycle pump. Like this. (*he demonstrates*)

Hanif: Yes, thank you very much. Would you mind popping into the Waiting Room (*to Mushtaq*) I'll call the next group in. (*They arrive*)

Mushtaq: Do, please sit down. Now we've been looking at your entry. Perhaps you could describe it to us.

E: We only want the very best resting place for our beloved Pharaoh. Tell them, F.

F: It's a tube. An extended cylinder. Like a cigarette or a pencil.

Hanif: Neither of which have been invented yet!

E: Excuse me but I drew these plans with a pencil.

F: So it must have been invented.

Mushtaq: Oh, alright. Tell us, which way will the – tube – lie?

E: We thought it could be like this. – so that the Pharaoh can look up and see all the sky where he will one day be in control.

Hanif: But when he uses it the Pharaoh will be dead.

F: Yes, I warned you about that E!

E: (*floundering*) We could pop him inside – or it could be a gun.

Mushtaq: Yes. Well thank you very much for the moment. Please wait outside. Hanif – next please.

Not a brilliant morning so far (*next team arrives*)

Mushtaq: Now we are very keen to hear your story. Hello, I'm Mushtaq by the way. Go ahead.

G:	We're very excited.
H:	It's the result of many years' work.
G:	And study.
H:	By both of us. It's like a huge doughnut.
Mushtaq:	Doughnut?
G:	You know – a doughnut.
Hanif:	What is a doughnut?
H:	It's like a ring. One big circle and inside a smaller circle. You can eat it. Like this (*shows*) So we have a doughnut upright and Pharaoh's body is held in the centre. Like a bicycle wheel, really. Then we are going to ask our transport partners to invent a way it could be pulled round the kingdom.
G:	So everyone can see it. We've brought J along as he's an expert on wheels. J!
J:	I think it's a silly idea. I've told them that lots of times. We've only got camels and I haven't invented a motor car with a tow bar, yet. It could be years away.
H:	Oh, you've really let us down J.
G:	I thought you would come up with a good idea, J.
J:	Well, I did tell you. I haven't even finished inventing the spanner yet.
Mushtaq:	Well, gentlemen. No bad feelings please. Could you just wait outside, for a few moments. Hanif, I think there's one team still waiting. (*they enter*)
K:	Good morning. L – it's Pharaoh's tombs today.
L:	I'll get the papers out K.

Mushtaq: Now we've looked at this hard and long. Explain it to my colleague and I. I have to say, we're not very happy.

K: We realise this is a little unusual and unconventional but we think a pyramid is the best answer. For such a tomb.

Hanif: Well, to me it looks very dangerous. It could easily fall over. In a sandstorm, etc.

L: If I dare say so, you have got the plan upside down.

Hanif: Oh, sorry.

K: The pyramid sits on its square side, in the sand.

Hanif: Like this (*he demonstrates*)

K: Like that.

Mushtaq: But it is about 100 metres high. However could you make it?

L: That's my concern. At first we thought we could make it of concrete but our enquiries showed that that hasn't been invented yet. So we chose stone. We would get a huge cube of stone and cut it into shape. Luckily – except for them, of course - we have a large pool of labour and they have agreed – sort of – to have a go. What we do is cut four big slices off and that leaves a suitable tomb for the Pharaoh.

Hanif: What about the four pieces?

L: I was coming to that. They would make smaller pyramids – for Pharaoh's children. When they die, of course. Or we could sell them – as souvenirs.

Mushtaq: Well, you've made your case. We'd be grateful if you would join the others in the Waiting Room until we reach a decision. (*K and L withdraw. Hanif and Mushtaq confer. They all return*)

Mushtaq: Well first of all thank you all for coming. Designing a Pharaoh's tomb does not come along every day. We've decided not to make a choice today. The Pharaoh kindly rang us and told us he was feeling fairly well. So, we'll spend some time thinking about your ideas. We thought the sphere idea was a good one. It would both look good and attract tourists for many years. The cylinder deserves more consideration and the symbolism of it doubling as a telescope is most interesting. We haven't got one of those. We liked the doughnut idea with its theme of circulation but we feel more thought will have to go into taking it round the country. And will it go stale?

Alas, the team submitting the pyramid will have to go back to the drawing board. It just wouldn't work and we calculate that to cut the stone into the right shape would take at least two months and would use 17 saws which no-one has invented yet. Besides the Pharaoh wants to see it before he – goes. And he's fine at the moment.
Sorry K & L.

Any questions?

'VISITORS'

A group of about ten space 'characters' come on stage. Chatting to each other and clearly excited. Some a little unsteady on their 'feet'. One of them, the leader, steps forward.

L: Right. You have all learnt to stand. Now, so that we can talk please form a straight line. (*They form a perfect semi-circle*). I said 'Line'. You must have missed that English class! But that will do.

Now a quick role call: x47, x55, x201, y30, y8, t6, t7 and t8, z1.

(*They answer as called*)

It all is very quiet. I don't know where the earthmen are. But that gives us a chance to make a good survey.

Some points: We landed here because we saw some signs of earthman's life. We are to stay friendly with anyone we meet. Don't forget we have the problem of getting back home again and we need their help to do that. Look around carefully as you all did in your training. In 7 zedas time we will meet back here – with anything you can find. Any questions?

X201: What do we do if they own things we find?

L: Ask them if we can borrow them for our research.

T6: Do we pay them?

L: What is the point? They have the money. We have other ways of paying. They couldn't use ours could they?

T8: But it was a good question, wasn't it?

All: (*Murmur – 'yes' or 'no'*)

L: Right, off you go. You can work in pairs or singly. *(The group goes off in various directions).*

Scene 2

(7 zedas later. The group assembles slowly. Carrying the things they have collected).

L: Now, how was it? Firstly, did anyone meet an earthman – see any signs of an earthman?

X55: I saw some footprints, L.

L: Did you bring any measurements back?

X55: No. I was too busy looking for objects – things….

L: Well, what have you got there?

X55: It's two – pots *(cruets)*. But I don't know what they are for.

L: Let me see *(L looks at them)* Ah, yes, let me see *(L consults catalogue)* Yes. They hold a kind of perfume. One is for people who are white and the other for those who are black. Did you know that earthman is not like us? They can choose to be either white or black. Sometimes other colours too. Well done X55! We'll take those back with us. Funny people earthmen. You have to turn these upside down to use them. Like this. *(They all laugh)* Now – who found other things? Y30.

Y30: I found this *(produces an egg)*.

L: *(taking it carefully)* Hey. What a stroke of luck. Do you know what this is? *(they don't)*. Well it is known as an igg. No-one has ever found one before. On Space Mission Delta they spent a lot of time looking. An igg. Within this igg is a baby earthman. One day he will break out of this igg and become what they call 'a person'. Now isn't it amazing. Within this little shell, this igg, is a baby earthman.

X201: Can we touch it?

L: No, sorry. It is far too important. Just wait till we get home and tell the laboratories about this. Maybe they will be able to develop it. I'm told it takes 275 zedas to do that. Y30 – well done! Any more?

Y30: I found this, L. *(hands over a coffee machine – cafetiere)*

L: We must handle this carefully. It is an earthman's weapon. We think – we don't really know – but we think this is from earthman's military. The glass is full of explosives – that is material that blows up – and when this knob is pressed down, well, then, it 'blows up'. And it can hurt many earthmen or many of us. We don't have anything like that – do we?

All: No, L.

X47: L, I was looking for something else when I found this. *(hands over some boy's underpants)*.

L: Thank you x47. Earthmen uses these for keeping his teapot cold. You see the handle fits in there; and the spout fits in there. These have been thrown away because there's no place to put in the water – liquid to you and me. What else have you there X47?

At this point, two of the group can present an object and L can try to find a (wrong) use for it. The others all believe L who is 'the expert')

L: Very good – so far. Now it is chargetime. Please take a place for 4 zedas charge. *(group in pairs sit back-to-back. Something like sleep).*

X201: *(While the others are 'charging' – sleeping)*

L, can I ask your advice, please? How do we start living?

L: We think there are two kinds of human –

X201: Black and white?

L: No. Man and non-man. When they are about quarter old, man meets a non-man. They do something together but we don't really know what. And then later the non-man lays an igg – just like the one that Y30 found. Somehow they warm the igg and after about 270 to 280 zedas a little earthman appears.

X201: From inside the igg?

L: Yes! Now that earthman can be an earth non-man. Say a wo-man.

X201: Wo-man. But a little wo-man?

L: Yes. Like us it has to grow – get bigger.

X201: Then earth people go to a shop and choose one of these. Sometimes more.

We're not made like that, are we.

L: You'll find out. When you get bigger!

Y8: *(as they 'wake')* L, when you talked about the igg, I was very interested.

L: Yes. Y8 how do you think we grow? I've just been talking to X201 about that.

Y8: Well. There is a farm on our planet and the farmer grows certain things. Then the farmer picks them and churns them all together in a big pot and we come out – once we are heated. By the sun.

L: Good. Now earthmen go to a special shop and see little earthmen on the shelf and they can choose which one they want. And they buy it.

Y30: Buy it?

L: Yes or swap it for something they think is precious. Something very valuable.

Z1: Is this a precious thing, L? *(produces an umbrella)*

L: VERY precious, Z1. You watch. *(opens umbrella)*. You may think this is for catching water. Or protecting yourself against the warm.

Y8: I thought it was for defending yourself if you got attacked, L.

L: No, no *(he takes Z1 aside and explains the use of an umbrella to Z1. Meanwhile the rest take X201 aside and demand to know what L told him).*

Several: Go on X201. Tell us what he said. What did he tell you, etc.?

X201: Well, he said that an earthman and a non-earthman – he called a wo-man – get together and lay an igg. When it is warm it becomes a little earthman – something like that.

X47: Rubbish! You would believe anything, X201! Remember this, I came on the last trip and saw a book, written in English. It said that earthman and earthwoman lived together – and soon a big bird came, carrying a small earthling. And then it said that sometimes the earthling is found – under a gooseberry bush!

L: What are you lot doing? Come on – we have to leave soon. Did anyone else find anything?

T7: I found this white thing. On a rubbish tip. What is it L?

L: *(Looking through)* Well, this is interesting. I must look up my little book *(does so)*. Ha! Yes. Here you see it says TV and Radio. I can see what it is – it is the plan by which all earth people must live. They have to read this every day to know how to live, how to behave. Excellent. Maybe we will be able to copy some of their plans and ideas. Wouldn't it be wonderful if we had TV?

All: And radio….

L: Look here. It tells you how the people in Australia behave. And here – it tells you what the weather will be. And how to be a policeman. Here it shows you how to be a millionaire. When I was young we were told that the earthman had a book called a bible but this must have replaced it…….. Any more objects? We've certainly found some good ones.

Y8: L, I don't know what this is. I found it near a house. *(a football)*

L: Ah, that is for carrying water. You see it is made of strong skin and is waterproof. You fill it with water – there. And you can carry it back to your home. From the river or the lake.

(At this point the rest of the class come on as a team – dressed possibly in football gear)

P: Look lads, there it is. Excuse me but what are you doing with our football? Eh?

L: Football? Won't the water all spill out?

P: We are in the middle of a game. Give it back? Who are you anyway?

L: We are visitors, trying to find out how you earthmen live.

P: Come on then. Make a team. Like us. Fred, blow your whistle. *(they begin to kick the ball).*

L: Hey, stop. All the water will spill out of it. No, stop, what are you doing, etc. *(as lights fade).*

'BABY SITTER'

CAST:

Alan Jackson

Joy Jackson

Jennie

Mike

Beverley

Scene 1: (A suburban house)

Alan:	Guess!
Joy:	I can't
Alan:	Go on, guess.
Joy:	Knowing you it could be anything.
Alan:	Maybe.
Joy:	Has old Campbell given you promotion?
Alan:	Good idea – but no. Try again.
Joy:	You've won the Lottery?
Alan:	That's a good idea. No! Last chance.
Joy:	Give up. Come on Alan, I haven't all day to spare. Bev's upstairs and she'll be awake by now.
Alan:	Think tonight. Clue: Think THEATRE!
Joy:	What?
Alan:	I've rung up and booked two tickets for the opera tonight, at The Dukes.

Joy: Alan, I'm really grateful but – you know I don't think I like opera. 'Carmen' is the only one I've ever liked and that was on the telly.

Alan: You'll never believe this but – 'Carmen' it is. Two Dress Circle tickets. Aren't you happy?

Joy: Yes, of course. I have always wanted to see it on stage.

Alan: And, wait for it, Katherine Fuente is singing Carmen.

Joy: But what about Bev, darling?

Alan: That's next.

Joy: I know the Newsteads are away. Let's try Jennie. I'll give Betty a bell. Just wait a minute. You see to Bev....,

Scene 2:

Joy: That'll be them.

Alan: O.K. *(Goes to door)* Just coming! Hello, Jennie.

Jennie: Oh – er. Hi, Mr Jackson.

Alan: Come in. What's it like out? Coats needed?

Jennie: Yes...... I think......

(Small pause)

Alan: Well – aren't you going to make the necessary introduction?

Jennie: Oh, yea. This is Mike, Mr Jackson.

Alan: Hello Mike. Do you.... er.... live around here?

Mike: Oh, hi! I go to the....er..... Poly, with Jen. Yea.

Alan: *(Calling upstairs)* Joy – it's Jennie come to babysit; and.... er.....

Mike: Mike Russell.

Joy: Coming darling. Beverley, get your slippers on darling. *(Awkward pause)*

Alan: Well we're off to the play, Jennie. Joy's probably told you. We should be back by elevenish.

Joy: Hello, you two. Beverley, this is Jennie. Do you remember her? She's a bit shy, Jennie.

Mike: *(To Jennie)* Can we…..er….sit down.

Alan: Oh, this is Mike by the way darling. Jennie's man!

(No reaction) He's at the Poly too. Now Jennie, we're at the Dukes Theatre and there's –

(Beverley begins to cry – attaches herself to mother)

Joy: Sorry about this Jennie. Usually no problem.

(Beverley clings and gets 'in a state')

Alan: Come on Bev. You said you'd be good if Mummy and Daddy went out. Come on – here Jenny – take her….

Beverley: Don't go…. Don't go….. Mummy….. Mummy.

Joy: Well – I must say – Alan we'll have to watch the time – I'll pop upstairs with her. Maybe she's over-tired. *(Goes)*

Alan: Jennie – what's up? She knows you well and she's been chatting about you all day.

Mike: You go, Mr m…m…m – she'll be O.K. Jennie'll fix her I bet.

Alan: Just you two wait there *(He goes upstairs to Joy)*. Joy! Put Bev down, darling. Now listen: the child's done it. I thought they both looked pretty dopey when they came in.

Joy: They're not a bit drunk, darling. How awful. Whatever set Bev off like that?

Alan: That's the point. I got a whiff just now. It isn't alcohol. Worse. They're high on drugs.

Joy: Alan – Oh God! What shall we do – poor Jennie.

Alan: Poor Beverley – poor us. And poor tickets *(tearing up theatre tickets)*. I've got to ring Jennie's mother, Joy.

Joy: No, wait, let's think….oh, dear…. Beverley – off to sleep; don't worry, darling, we won't leave you…..

Alan: What's Betty's number?

Joy: Wait, darling – let's think…….

'GETTING AHEAD'

CAST

The head   - Gary

The body   - Ronnie

Nurse

Visitors (4) – Dad, Mum, Annie, Robert

Surgeon's team (4)

The scene depicts a single bed in a hospital ward. Besides the bed itself one needs a bedside cupboard (carefully designed) and perhaps four hospital chairs. Hospital atmosphere can be created with perhaps some medical apparatus, a clipboard plus graphs etc.

The body in bed simply lacks a head! In the situation where you can't find an actor thus endowed use a headed actor and dress him/her as if the body stops at the neck. The head is played by an actor who can be hidden, at first, in the bedside cupboard; eventually the head appearing through the top. Thus:

As the lights fade up the audience is given a few seconds to take in the situation – before a nurse appears. She is going to give the patient in bed a wash and general clean up – tidy the bed, tries to provide water but realises this is futile etc. This action can take place over perhaps three minutes. Possibly the nurse can chat to the patient but she will get few verbal replies. Maybe some other body-language!

A group of visitors (family?) enter and look for this bed. They too talk to the body but with little contact. Finding chairs, when three sit one side of the bed and one on the other.

Mum: Ronnie. How are you?

Dad: Frances. He can't answer. Not yet. I think he looks better than he did, don't you Annie?

Annie: Considering his situation, yes I do.

Robert: Ron. Put up some fingers to tell us when you expect the transplant.

(Body raises one finger)

Robert: Tomorrow. Any idea who <u>it</u> will be? We need to know in case we visit you tomorrow. Who to look out for. *(Body does elaborate mime, with hands).*

Mum: He says he will be the one in yellow jimjams. Ronnie we think you're very brave. What do you think?

Dad: Frances *(nudges)* Ronnie can't think – until tomorrow.

Annie: Perhaps it doesn't matter. We've brought you some little goodies, Ron. These are from 'Four Seasons' – just some grapes. To help you get ahead.

(Ronnie rejects the grapes as he has nowhere to put them).

Oh, sorry Ronnie, I forgot. Mum, dad – some grapes?

Robert: I suppose they are waiting for spare head, Ron. Will it be male or female? I hope it's a male as I've always wanted a brother.

(Ronnie draws that it will be a male. The whole family clap)

Dad: I've brought your ciggies, Ron.

Mum: I told you Ron had promised to give up smoking after the accident, Jack. Here's 'The Rover'. *(Hands over local paper with Ronnie turns over the pages with little interest).*

Nurse: Please don't move. Just the daily rounds.

Surgeon: This is Mr *******. What do you notice Dr Trill?

Trill: Right hip, Mr Vince?

Surgeon: No, try again. Dr Goodheart?

Dr Goodheart: It must be something to do with his head. I wouldn't know how to tackle that.

Surgeon: Frankly, neither do I. This is my first 'topping' as we call it. Luckily a replacement has just arrived – strangely enough from another motor cycle accident. Mr *****, tomorrow we'll have you up and smiling. Any questions?

(Ronnie makes an elaborate mime)

Surgeon: No. No eating until we tell you. Hope the new head has an appetite. Thank you nurse. Next, please. *(They move off)*

Mum: A nice man. Did you notice his lovely hands, Ron. No, of course you didn't.

Robert: I'd like to sing you a little song I wrote for you, Ron. Listen carefully:

Everyone knows you're a long time dead

You've got a big heart and now you need a head.

Soon you'll look and listen; soon you'll be fed

Our old Ron is getting ahead.

(They all join in. But Ron doesn't respond. Weak clapping).

(Nurse arrives, carrying what looks like a dome from a silver service with a thin board underneath it. She smiles at the visitors and places it carefully on the bedside table).

Nurse: There. A little surprise for you and a big one for you *(to Ronnie)* Now let's sing the last two lines of Ronnie's song *(they do – mystified)* Now, Sapristi! *(She removes the cover, revealing the Head).*

Mum: Oh, that's lovely. Ron. Do you like it?

Dad: Didn't shave this morning, did you Ronnie?

Annie: That's not Ronnie, dad. Yet. Tomorrow, maybe.

Robert: Hello. I'm Robert. You're going to be my brother. Well, half brother.

Head: Yes. So they say. Is this my body?

Robert: No. That's Ronnie, my brother's body. Mum I think we should go now and let these two – halves – get together. Nurse what happens if they don't – don't get on?

Nurse: They will. Once Mr Vince gets going.

Dad: Head. What's your name?

Head: I suppose it will be Ronnie. It used to be Gary but after the accident I lost just about everything.

Annie: Well, you'll love Ronnie. In fact you'll be Ronnie, won't you?

Robert: We've got to go. Ronnie – what do you think?

(Ronnie makes some desperate signs, with his arms)

Robert: Ron says, "Leave the grapes mum, and the ciggies dad".

(They do, taking them to Head who can use them. The family make to go.)

Mum: *(To Head)* We hope you'll be very happy. Dad won't it be nice to have a real conversation. Bye Ronnie, love. Best wishes for 'the topping'.

Dad: We'll be thinking of you tomorrow. And we hope you'll be thinking – of us.

Annie: Goodbye, Gary. Just for one more day. *(They go).*

Nurse: *(entering. She washes Gary. And Ronnie squirms. Ronnie takes up 'The Rover' paper and tries to read it. Eventually passes it over to Gary who needs Ronnie's hands to hold it, turns the pages etc.).*

'NEWCOMERS'

CAST

Alan	Mr Skinner
Brian	Brenda
Gary	Mandy
Fred	Felicity
Pete	Bruin
Pozzo	
Benny	

(The scene is a football changing room. The building is small and run-down. Four footballers are there in various stages of changing for a match).

Scene 1

Alan: What did you do at half-term, lads?

Brian: Not much. I went to see Palace play – they lost.

Alan: Forgotten how to win!

Gary: Had to help me dad paint the house – the sitting room.

Alan: Boring. Did you get any of the paint on the walls?

Gary: Look here *(shows hands with paint)* The rest went on the walls.

Fred: *(of few words)* Mmmmm. Yea…… yea….. mmmmm.

Alan: Where are the others? He wasn't very happy with the last game. He said 14 – 0 was the most he'd ever had scored against one of his teams. He talked about 'changes'.

(Others arrive)

Pete and Pozzo:	Hey, everyone! *(they murmur, 'hello')*. What are we playing seven-a-side?
Alan:	The chance would be a good thing. There's only six of us.
Gary:	Old skin head said there would be changes – maybe he thinks we can win with six.
Alan:	This team couldn't win with sixty.
Pozzo:	Just because we lost 14 – 0. They were professionals.
Fred:	From St Benedict's……?
Pete:	That's for handicapped kids.
Fred:	I know – I used to go there.
Brian:	What – did they throw you out, Fred?
Fred:	Yes. They said I wasn't handicapped but headicapped.
All:	*(they laugh)*
Benny:	*(arrives breathless)* Had to run all the way from the bus-stop. Where's Skinhead?
Gary:	And now you've got to run for ninety minutes more. Or we're in trouble. Al, have you noticed anything?
Alan:	What – there's only seven of us?
Gary:	Nick told me Skinner was thinking of selling off some of us. Perhaps he's sold Jamie – and Grant.
All:	*(They all stop changing and silence hits the changing room)*
Alan:	He wouldn't – would he?
Brian:	He couldn't – we've got no reserves. Fred, <u>you</u> only got in to make the numbers up to eleven.

Fred:	You shut up! You too!
All:	*(Argument breaks out – some for Fred, some against. In walks Mr Skinner. They all jump to attention)*
Skinner:	Fred: remember?
Fred:	Can't untie this knot Mr Skinner.
Skinner:	Didn't you bring your mummy, Fred?
Fred:	She can't play football.
Skinner:	I have news for you – neither can her son!
Fred:	Who, my brother?
Skinner:	No – <u>his</u> brother. Now listen lads. I've had to make certain changes.
Alan:	I don't want to play centre half Mr Skinner.
Gary:	Are we changing to rugby Mr Skinner?
Brian:	Listen everyone, to Mr Skinner. We're facing relegation.
Skinner;	That would normally be true Brian but as you may have noticed we're in the bottom league – nowhere to go. This is my plan. With the local transfer market opening up Jamie, Fairfax, Grant and Smithie have decided to go elsewhere. I managed to transfer them for £40 which will immediately be spent on improving this place. The leaking roof, etc. Come in *(he goes to the door and beckons in four girls)*

	And I managed to get these lovely ladies free – so we have a team, after all. And no-one is keener than Brenda, Mandy, Felicity and Bruin. *(He introduces them to the alarm of the seven boys)*
Fred:	What about changing Mr Skinhead?
Skinner:	Skinner, Fred! Well, you boys come down this end and the girls can normally change that end.
Brian:	This is terrible Mr S. Don't mind losing Jamie and company half as much – but girls! Football.
Brenda:	I've been playing for six months. And scored 27 goals.
Fred:	We've only scored 22 in two seasons, Brian. Anyway I like girls.
Gary:	Yes – but not playing football.
Skinner:	Now lads – take it or leave it. What else could I do: 14 – 0!
	Anyway, we play in three minutes. So get on with it.
	The new rules state that you can have a mixed team. And you were mixed even before I found these lovely ladies.
Gary:	But I think it will be difficult tackling them, Mr S.
Skinner:	They are on <u>your</u> side, Gary. You tackle the others – the opposition.
Brian:	Who are we playing today Mr S? They'll laugh at us.
Skinner:	No, I don't think so. We're playing the newcomers – St Angelina's. All girls, Brian.

Brian: That sounds better!

Skinner: Oh, so you don't mind girls playing football, Brian?

Brian: Don't mind playing <u>against</u> them, we might actually win – but I don't like playing <u>with</u> them.

Skinner: Now, here's the team:

      Goal   -   Felicity

      Back four - Pete, Pozzo, Brian and Gary

      Midfield - Benny, Fred, Bruin

      Up front - Brenda, Mandy, Alan

On the bench – me. Is that all clear?

Fred: Shall I hang back, with Bruin, Mr S?

Skinner: You leave her alone. You take St Angelina's forward on the right and mark her.

Fred: How shall I mark her?

Skinner: Like you should have done when we lost 14 – 0.

Felicity: Is my make-up alright Desmond?

Brian: Who's Desmond, for heaven's sake?

Skinner: That's me. You call me Mr Skinner, Brian.

That's lovely Felicity. Makes you feel good. Now don't forget Felicity, you're a goalkeeper not a ballet dancer. Try to catch the ball cleanly.

Felicity: Can I use my hands, Desmond?

Gary: Your hands!!!?

Felicity: I used other means last time – waggled me hips and the forward shot straight over the bar.

Pete: I can't believe it?

Brenda: Look here. Last time <u>you</u> played you let 14 goals in. The team we all played for used to win by that margin. So shut up and get on with the game.

Fred: We can't be relegated Mr Skinner said.

Brenda: You <u>are</u> ambitious – you lot. Right off we go – best of luck everyone.

Fred: I'll mark the Mother Superior.

Brian: St Angelina's is not a convent, Fred, it's a women's prison.

(They go off to the match)

Fred: Hope me hair's OK. What do you think Brian?

Brian: Get walking Fred………

Scene 2 *(The group/team returns to the dressing room after the game. They are all very depressed and quiet. No-one speaks for about a minute. They change. Skinner isn't there).*

Alan: It could have been worse.

Gary: How?

Alan: We all could have been sent off.

Pete: I wish I was. I'm thinking of retiring.

Alan: How can you retire when you're fourteen?

Pete: Taking up chess or something. I must have run about 5 kilometres without touching the ball.

Pozzo: They were good – for girls.

Brenda: It was our fault, was it? I didn't get a single pass all afternoon.

Fred: Come on – it was better than our last game.

Pete: It couldn't be worse. Fourteen – Nil!

Benny: Where's His Majesty?

Pete: He stayed behind to talk to their coach.

Felicity: I'm really sorry everyone. I had the ball then Brian banged into me and I dropped it. That blonde girl was always goal-hanging.

Brian: Don't worry Felicity. Our goalie in the last game dropped about five of them. And he didn't see five more.

Skinner: Well done. Fourteen – Nil down to one nil. We're improving. I wonder what made the difference?

Pete: We tried harder because we didn't want to look stupid in front of the girls

Skinner: Which girls?

Pete: Theirs – and ours. I thought Brenda tried really hard. Brenda – I'm giving up football. It hurts too much. Are you doing anything tonight? *(they talk aside).*

Fred: Yeah. Good idea. Brian – are you doing anything tonight?

Brian: Ask one of <u>them</u> *(indicates the other girls).*

Skinner: Well. We've got another game on Tuesday and if Pete is going I'll have to bring Rosie. Lovely little girl – excellent down the wing.

Brian: More women?

Skinner: Yes. She comes out of nick (prison) on Monday. Wants to start a new life…….

Pozzo: I'm ball-boy this week. Where's the ball. *(No-one has it)*

Alan: Hey, I saw one of St Angelina's after the game – and she was a funny shape…….

'STEPHEN JONES – THIS IS YOUR LIFE'

Casting

Bill MC1	(Presenter of Programme)
Rachel MC2	(Presenter of Programme)
Hilary Jones	(Stephen's Mother)
David Jones	(Stephen's Father)
Chuck Grant	
Alex Coundell	
Gavin	(Researcher)
Dave Paxton	
Tanya La Rue	
Other Researchers	

'STEPHEN JONES -TIYL'

MC1: Ladies and gentlemen, boys and girls, I think you know the programme and the form it takes. And of course you all know Stephen Jones – this week's star of 'This is your Life'.

Even now Stephen is on his way here to the studio. And of course we have arranged it so that he doesn't know why he's coming. He <u>thinks</u> he is coming to discuss a sponsorship, advertising football boots.

But, like you, we have a surprise for him.
Soon all these empty chairs will be filled – by you, for you are the people closest to Stephen and today the TV audience of several million will find out how you have all become important in Stephen's life and indeed in his success.

MC2: We have just over five minutes for a quick practice. First then I'm calling on Hilary and David Jones, Stephen's parents. Bill –

MC1: Hilary and David, what kind of boy was Stephen?
(Bill)

Hilary: Well – a lovely lad, really. Always ambitious but helping in the house; very much enjoying holidays with us – you know.

MC1: Good………

David: He was very shy as a little boy and followed the others rather then –

MC1: Yes I'm sorry to stop you there but we only have a few minutes left.

MC2: I'm calling Chuck Grant.

MC1:	Hi Chuck. By the way, Hilary and David, you take those seats there during the programme. They are marked. Back to you, Chuck. Quickly now, tell us what school was like – you were great friends in those days?
Chuck:	Stephen was usually very well behaved. But we did get up to some – well, tricks.
MC2:	That's about all there's time for now. Chuck – sit over there when the programme is on. Remember the tricks! Now we have to tell you that our Special Guest – who will fill the last seat there – is Amy whom we've flown in from Australia. Keep that one quiet, of course. Next – Alex Coundell. Alex – up you come. Bill.
MC1:	Hello Alex. Alex Coundell was Stephen's guitar teacher. How good was he, Alex?
Alex:	Oh, he had lots of potential. I think he could have done very well. But the football was his first love and he simply couldn't put in the time – on the guitar.
MC2:	We're getting a message that Stephen is held up in a bit of traffic. At this point as we have a little time we'd like to introduce you to Gavin our Head of Research.
Gavin:	Hello. Yes I'm sure you know that 'This is Your Life' is very much about research. And on this occasion it has to be kept as a tight secret – as you'll all know best. Without your help and agreement we simply would not have a programme. Our target is to have Stephen come through that door – totally surprised. Nearly always the subject (Stephen) joins in but we record the programme just in case. We'd all look very silly if our 'life' suddenly ran away! And one or two have tried.

Jill:	Stephen helped us quite a lot without knowing it. His book "Two Feet on the Ground" helped us and we have lots of newspaper clips and video film too. We would like to thank you for joining in the spirit of this programme. People have said it 'invades privacy' and even cheats but we don't think so. Stephen Jones is a public figure and in the future both he and you will look back on tonight's programme with great pleasure. And we hope six million other people will too.

Perhaps you should meet a few of my research team. I think you will know some of them.

(3 or 4 step forward) |
MC2:	Alex – that one is your seat when we start. Let's try Dave Paxton. Dave come on up.
MC1:	Hello Dave. Now when did you first think Stephen was on the road to fame?
Dave:	The lad showed great talent, great skill from the start. I spotted him playing for his school team. The group were up to 16 years old but Stephen was in the first team at 13. Well, nearly 14. That all seems ages ago – about 6 years ago. What I was -
MC1:	Sorry to stop you. Keep the interesting bits in when we are broadcasting the programme. Thanks, Dave. Next?
MC2:	This will have to be the last. Tanya La Rue please. Hurry now.
MC1:	Now Miss La Rue. May I call you Tanya. Yours is a very interesting story – how did you meet Stephen Jones?

Tanya: Yes – it was like this. I was in the High Street when someone driving a BMW came speeding down the road. Stephen wasn't looking and stepped out and the car hit him.

MC1: And thanks to you, you called Emergency and an ambulance came and Stephen was in hospital within minutes. Thanks to you Stephen got immediate attention which not only saved his life but also his football career.

Tanya: Yes, we're good friends now.

MC2: Right. Now listen everyone. Stephen is on his way. All those who have been rehearsing with my colleague please go that way to the waiting area where another colleague will look after you. Now do hurry please. Remember we want just yourselves on stage – no luggage, parcels, handbags. And no mobile phones, please. Good luck!

MC1: Here we go Rachel (*to MC2*). Cross your fingers. This should be a good one. Just check that Amy's OK. She might be just a bit jet-lagged.

2 minutes later

Stephen Jones is shown into the studio.

Stephen Jones: Through here, did you say?

Jill: Yes – now turn right.

MC1: (*meeting Stephen*): I wonder if I could have a word with you, Mr Jones? I'm a sports journalist and I wonder – "Stephen Jones, this is your life!"

Stephen Jones: (*realising that the game is up*): Not on your life. Goodbye! (*He runs off, leaving his friends behind.*)

MC1: After him – quickly!

Chuck: You don't know Stephen – or what it would take to catch him!

MC2: Now listen everyone – stay back there – listen. Stephen didn't want to be filmed and he's made off.

At this news all rise from their chairs, go towards the stage and make a noisy protest.

This text allows the cast the chance to add perhaps two more characters, such as the Manager of Stephen's club or his national team. It can then be played with Stephen there – going through the list as during rehearsal.

'WITNESSES'

Cast:

Detective Sergeant
Police Constable Tom Egan
Police Woman Constable Jennie Jones
Mrs Adams
Bill Panton
Gladys Richfield
James Lester
Anthea Silk
Fazal Shima
Reverend Baxter

Someone has been killed in a traffic accident. The police interview several witnesses. Their evidence makes a car driver appear to be the guilty party. But eventually the truth presents itself.

As with the other plays space can be left for students to create their own witnesses. These students will probably be from the 'fast track'. They can write their own words or, better still, improvise them. This means, of course, that PC Egan also has to improvise. The best place for this to be included is probably after the three police have met – mid play.

Interviews can be recorded as the police do – on cassette. Another scene could be devised to let those in the waiting room talk about their experience.

A mature class could be asked to write variations on Julia Grant's final note.

Detective Sergeant: (*As the group take their seats*) Just a few words. Thank you very much for coming today. We need your help and you have all responded by coming here and agreeing to help us.

This case – of the death of a young woman – Julia Grant – is a very sad one and we in the Police share your sadness at her death – leaving three young children. In order to get good evidence we are going to talk to you one at a time. So if Mrs Adams could stay here with us would the others please go with PWC Jones and wait in the room next door – until we call you. Thank you – PWC Jones, can you make everyone some coffee? (*They all go with her*).

Now, Mrs Adams, if you sit at this desk my colleague will chat to you.

P.C.: Mrs Adams – here is a map of the street where the accident happened. Where were you at the time?

Mrs Adams: Now where is the park? I was sitting on a park seat at the time – waiting for my grandson to come out of school. It would be – about there. Well, I was looking in my handbag when I heard a big crash. I looked up and saw this woman lying in the road at the side of a big black car. It must have been speeding. Then people came from everywhere.

P.C.: I've got that down. Thank you Mrs Adams.

P.W.C.: Come with me Mrs Adams I'll bring the next, Tom.

Bill Panton: Is this right?

P.C.: Yes, come in. It is Mr W. Panton is it?

Bill Panton: Yes – usually called Bill!

P.C.: Now Mr Panton, look at this little map. Where were you when the accident happened?

Bill Panton: Well, I was cycling down from the church when I saw this crowd of people – in the road. I had to get off my bike as the Ambulance came through – with its siren blaring. I put my bike by a street light and went to see what had happened but I couldn't get near so I left. Then a policeman came up to me and asked what I had seen. He took my name and address…..

P.C.: Yes, thanks Mr Panton. Next please. Mrs Richfield. Mrs Gladys Richfield.

Gladys: Yes. I'm Gladys Richfield.

P.C.: I'm just going to ask you a few questions, Mrs Richfield. Here's a map of the area. Where were you when the accident took place?

Gladys: I was in the butchers. I had nearly finished my order when we were all stopped by the sound of a crash outside. I was near the door so I popped out and there was a crowd in the middle of the road and a huge Bentley across the road. Those big cars shouldn't be allowed in my opinion – especially at the speed they travel.

P.C.: Yes – well thank you Mrs Richfield.

P.W.C.: James Lester.

P.C.: Come in Mr Lester and sit down please. By the way, how old are you Mr Lester?

Lester: I'm sixteen. Seventeen next birthday.

P.C.: Well I'm not sure if the Coroner will accept this – but here goes. Here's a map of the area where Mrs Grant was killed. Where were you?

Lester: Well, I was just off the map. There – there's a bit of Kimberley Close, leading on to the High Street. I heard this big bang and ran down to – to there.

P.C.: But that's about 200 metres from the accident.

Lester: Yes. But lots of people were running down to just by 'The Harvest Moon', the bakers. I didn't go with the crowd as I – I might have been in the way.

P.C.: Thanks Mr Lester. Off you go now. Next!

P.W.C.: Anthea Silk. This way – take my arm Miss Silk. You sit there and my colleague will talk to you.

P.C.: What happened Miss Silk – I know you're blind.

Anthea: I heard this car coming down the hill and suddenly there was a terrible screech of brakes and I knew something was wrong. When you can't see officer you know these things. Constable, as a blind person you know the car is your enemy. Poor Mrs Grant….

P.C.: Thank you for coming Miss Silk. Could you see her out Jennie? Next Fazal Shima. Come in Mr Shima.

Shima: Thank you. Excuse – English not good. Please.

P.C.: Mr Shima – where were you when this accident happened?

Shima: Were I am? Here. I here.

P.C.: No. Where were you? In what place?

Shima: What place? What is place – place??

P.C.: Here is a map – a map. Where were you?

Shima: Minton. Here Minton.

P.C.:	Yes, I know it's Minton. I live there too. Here is the park and here is the High Street. Where were you?
Shima:	Both.
P.C.:	Not both. Where? Show me.
Shima:	Here is Minton. Park. High Street. Halal butchers.
P.C.:	Last try Mr Shima. Accident. Bang. Woman killed. Where were you?
Shima:	Woman killed? Where.
P.C.:	This is useless. Have him back Jennie.
Shima:	"Have him back". Where is "useless"?

(Tom is alone in the interview room. In comes the Detective Sergeant and P.W.C. Jennie)

Det. Sgt.	How are you doing, Tom? You're pretty quick.
P.C.:	I'm getting nowhere. Lots of witnesses but none of their evidence would stand up in court. Those I've seem so far are living in a fantasy world. They were nowhere near the accident. But they <u>think</u> they were.
P.W.C.:	I thought they looked a nice bunch, Tom. All keen to help.
P.C.:	That's just the problem, Jennie. They want to help but they can't because they simply couldn't see what actually happened. Let's try again. The priest. Reverend Baxter please sit down. A few questions to try to find the circumstances of Julia Grant's death. Where were you at the time Mr Baxter? Here's a map if it helps.
Baxter:	No map. This is the middle of my parish, Constable. I was with a Mrs Wright an elderly lady whom I visit from time to time.
P.C.:	Where does she live - precisely?

Baxter:	Oh, on the third floor of that block – above the supermarket. I heard this bang and thought – another speeding car. Then ………
P.W.C.:	*(Enters)* Excuse me but could you come, Tom. Just one minute vicar. *(Outside)* I think we can let them all go Tom. There's been a development.
P.C.:	Yes. Not really much use these witnesses. None of them.
P.W.C.:	No – but its not that I'm afraid. Julia Grant's sister found this *(hands over letter)*
P.C.:	*(reads it out)* "Cis. I know you know I wasn't very well but things have changed. Dr Miller had sent me for a scan. I got the result today and it is the worst news. I have a tumour on my brain and it is so large that it is inoperable. All I can expect for the future is severe headaches and loss of control. I'm just off to the chemists for….. Love you" etc. etc.

Oh my God. I see what you mean. And that poor driver might well have been blamed. Terrible. Let them go, Jennie. Tell them "There have been developments". |
| **P.W.C.:** | And who tells those poor kids? |
| **P.C.:** | Best see the sister first Jennie…… |

'---- ING'

Three quarters of the play is shown here. The remaining quarter can be provided by, say, two 'fast track' students F & G who can prepare a scene of their own choice: once they have understood the idea of 'present continuous', as a developing and progressing idea. Depending on their talent and confidence their scenes would be either scripted or, preferably, improvised. Clearly their scene should not end the play.

From the text provided pairs of students should be simulating the action described by the commentator as Ann suggests. This should be planned in 'rehearsal' and it will surely add to the comic effect and also make more sense of the commentary itself.

CAST

Martin West		A Lecturer
Ann Felling		An assistant lecturer
B	}	
C	}	
D	}	
E	}	Student sports commentators
F	}	
G	}	
H	}	

Others working with B, C, D, E, F, G, H

A (Martin West): Welcome everybody. I'm Martin West and I'm in charge of this part of the course. We call this the 'ING' course and it is very important if you are hoping to be a sports commentator.

Now I'm going to ask you which sport you like best and which one you will be covering; and if you are working for television or radio. You first….. we are all listening!

B: I'm hoping to work on football. I'm thinking of going into TV.

A: Next.

C: I want to work on swimming and I'm expecting also to work for TV.

A: Thank you - next.

D: I'm trying to cover snooker – once again, for TV.

A: Thank you – and the next.

E: For many years I have been wanting to cover chess – for radio but also working on newspapers.

A: Many differing sports. Next.

F: Ice skating is my special interest. I'm hoping to cover that.

A: Lastly.

G: Cycling is my interest – both road racing and indoor track cycling.

A: Well there we are – six people, contrasting sports and wanting to work in differing media. H – who are you?

H: I'm just waiting.

A: Now here is what we want you to do. Each of you chooses an activity from everyday life. Then find two others to be practising doing this activity while you are giving an interesting commentary.

Over to Ann, my assistant. She will be helping you during this part of the course. Her name is Ann Felling so she's well qualified. Ann –

Ann: As Martin said, make a group of three. Name yourselves A, B and C.

B and C choose a simple everyday activity. I'll give you a list if you can't think of one. Then B and C <u>do</u> the activity – in mime – while A gives what we call 'a running commentary'. I'll show you – Martin *(Martin begins to wash face and then shave).*

Right "M is pouring some warm water into the basin. Now he's taking the soap and is washing his face. He's washing his neck and right up to his hair. Now he's rinsing his face – washing off the soapy water. Now he's reaching for his foam which is sitting on the shelf...." And so on! Do you understand?

Now make it sound like a good TV commentary – exciting so the person listening or watching doesn't turn off. Off you go! *(Groups of three are arranged. B starts)*

B: Welcome to Mr Jacob's studio where we are being allowed to watch him as he paints.

Now his assistant is setting up the canvas.... Mr J is choosing his paints..... now they are putting the butterfly near to the canvas.... and Mr J is starting. Now he's choosing a brush.... and he's starting now. He's using a blue, dark blue colour and he's starting on the butterfly's wings.... he's making a very big mark and filling maybe 30% of the canvas. Now he's asking for some water and now he's using a bigger brush and is spreading the colour. He's taking a little drink which the assistant is giving him... but wait.... now he's putting that canvas aside... he's taking another and he's starting again.....

A: Alright B. Very good. I was really wanting to see that painting – and what Mr J was doing. Why was he starting again? Next C, please.

C: *(The 'team' gets ready)*

If this is your first visit to a car-washing championship you are going to enjoy this. The competitors for the touring car section are getting their buckets of water and taking them to the car. They're putting one at the front and leaving one at the back.

The Judge is waving his flag and they're starting. John is starting on the roof while Jane is washing the tyres – they are using soapy water and cleaning the worst off with big sponges. Now John is washing the bonnet, throwing plenty of water. Jane is working on the boot....

A: Excellent C! You are making car-washing sound like something artistic! D next please.

D: An old lady is waiting at the side of the road. She's holding a white stick and is looking very nervous. Now I can see coming down the road two Boy Scouts both cycling. They see the old lady and they are talking together – they are stopping and putting their bikes against a tree. Now they are going up to the old blind lady – one of them is taking her right arm and one is taking her left arm. Now they are trying to lead her across the road. But she's refusing to go. She's trying to throw off their hands and – yes – she's shouting for help. She's free now but she's getting very angry. Now she's making for their bikes. They are trying to defend their bikes but she's hitting their bikes with her white stick. On dear. I think one wheel is coming off – now the other....

A: Right D just when it was getting exciting! Those poor lads – only trying to help. E – your turn.

E: Bill is going out – to a party and for some reason he's ironing his own shirt.

Now this is exciting. He's taking the ironing board and putting it up – in the kitchen. Now he's plugging in the iron and he's waiting for it to warm up. He's testing it with his finger – now he's trying a wet finger and if you're listening carefully you can hear the sizzling sound. Good – he's ready for the ironing. Now he's looking at his shirts and is deciding which one to choose. He's thinking, he's thinking. While he's deciding let's see what his mother is doing. Oh – yes – she's sitting watching television. But from time-to-time she's sleeping, nodding off.

Back to Bill who has taken a green shirt and we're going to watch him iron it… this is the kind of occasion when we wish you were watching with us. He's putting the sleeve…..

A: Yes – wish I was E. We won't ask why mother was not doing E's shirt. Now let's see how things are going.

(At this point bring in F and G – the ideas created by the students. Then A returns)

A: We're doing well. You are all getting…. Just one moment…. Something is happening *(a fire develops and H steps forward)*.

H: Now this is interesting…. Even exciting. Our teacher is having some small problems….smoke is coming from his pocket…. I'm afraid it's getting worse…. his whole body is now beginning to smoke…. he's trying to put it out… he's waving his arms and he's waving his legs…

but it's getting worse…. someone is trying to beat out the fire with a cushion… now he's running out of the room… one or two are following after him. Now he's outside and running towards the swimming pool…. which they are trying to fill up with water…. Ann is crying…. Martin is burning…. We are helpless just watching…..

'INCA THE THINKER'

PLAY – PERU 1530 a.d.

CAST:

Fuzco

Huelpa

Fuzco: Welcome back, Huelpa. Have a good trip?

Huelpa: Yes, boss, fantastic.

Fuzco: Where was it you went, now?

Huelpa: Oh, the other side – over the top.

Fuzco: Over the Andes. My word. Must have been quite a journey. What did you see?

Huelpa: Oh, it goes on and on and on – much bigger than here. I'll tell you about it. But how about here? It's good to be back. Any new inventions?

Fuzco: Well you can't have old ones my boy! We've had a marvellous time here. We missed you though. We've nearly managed the gold experiment. Remember – the one you started before you left?

Huelpa: Making gold from llama droppings?

Fuzco: Yes, that's the one. Nearly got there. And the earth experiment worked wonderfully – see here.

Huelpa: What's that boss?

Fuzco: It's a hoe, Huelpa. You use it for turning the soil. We've started on these *(shows 'fork')* but we mustn't rush at it.

Huelpa: That's great. But Fuzco, you should see what they've got over there –

Fuzco: Yes, yes, later boy.

Huelpa: They've got little things called 'coins'. You can use them to buy things. Gold 'coins', silver 'coins'…..

Fuzco: Well what's the use of that then? Why can't they just swap things, like we do? Did you tell them how we work – swapping? They probably haven't got that far – yet.

Huelpa: Yes, sort of. I didn't like to say too much.

Fuzco, can you keep a secret?

Fuzco: It depends what it is.

Huelpa: Listen to this. Everyone I met told me that the Spaniards were planning to come – to teach us about their God.

Fuzco: What are Spaniards, Huelpa? Are these the people with cons?

Huelpa: Coins, Fuzco. Yes, they are. And they like their coins very much. Nearly as much as their God.

Fuzco: Well, they'll never reach here. How would they get over our wonderful Andes mountains, Huelpa? Use your brain, lad. Anyway, we're building a fortress near Cuzco and they do say there will be a new town at Macchu Pichu…..

Huelpa: These Spaniards are very strong, Fuzco. They even kill their God. Then *(he whispers)*

Fuzco: Eat him, drink him. Are they animals?

Huelpa: Related. By the way, near where their God was born there's a country which suffers from terremoto, like us.

Fuzco: Terremoto. You mean *(he mimes an earthquake)*

Huelpa: Yes. And I got hold of a drawing which shows how they make their buildings so they won't fall down. Look here *(he shows sketch)*. See the angle?

Fuzco: We found that out long ago. I bet we have bigger terremoto than they do. When the Gods are angry. Wouldn't you be angry if they tried to kill you, then…… no, it's too much?

Huelpa: Have you heard of 'a play' Fuzco?? Well, near Spain is a country with a man who writes plays.

Fuzco: What do you mean 'writes'?

Huelpa: They've invented something called paper and then to remember these plays they make marks on the paper so they can remember it. Fantastic.

Fuzco: Can't they remember it without – whatever you said?

Huelpa: Writing.

Fuzco: Yes.

Huelpa: Well they're long plays. Maybe two porak long.

Fuzco: Too long. Wouldn't work here.

Well, anyhow, I'm into this now. Roof of house – rain – water stays. Roof of house – rain – water goes! How about that?

Huelpa: Great! But what if they want to collect water?

Fuzco: Collect water? With a damned great range of mountains in your back garden?

Huelpa: Oh, I see.

Fuzco: By the way, has llama got water?

Huelpa: I'll check. Fuzco, did you ever hear of a 'horse'?

Fuzco: Come again?

Huelpa: A 'horse'.

Fuzco: No. *(pause)* Now we've got the forester coming soon. We must get ready. He's got some brilliant idea – with log rollers.

Huelpa: Yes, that's it! I remember now. Fuzco, the most incredible thing I saw, in the whole trip. Look I did a drawing of it – like you said. Here…..

Fuzco: *(Inspects drawing).* H W E L……H E W L……

Huelpa: WHEEL, Fuzco. You see, they have these wheels. They put things on top of them – and pull people and things around on them. They roll!!!

Fuzco: *(Thinks – then)* It'd never work – too thin. They'd break.

Huelpa No, Fuzco, you're wrong. They're everywhere – streets , land, town, country. In machines. On transport. Moved by water.

Fuzco: Thin logs, e.g.? Now look here Huelpa. You've got to settle down to a sense of reality. You've had your trip. 'Coins', 'horses', 'wheels', - my God, you'll have them shooting things out of hollow tubes next! Now – coat off and start moving those old log rollers over here. Before the forester comes. Tut…. Tut…. Tut. No good sending you away….. sense of reality……feet on the ground……

MUSEUM

'LOOKING BACK'

CAST:

The Museum Director

Sandy

Eric

Miriam

Sebastian

Magnus Donovan

Jenny

Adrian

Antony

Mrs Verity

Scene 1:

Director: Now thank you for coming. I hope you know why you're here.

Sandy: Only ten days to go. Before <u>they</u> come and spoil it all!

Director: Well, some of you may think that funny but I have to remind you all that a museum without customers is…. is like…. A football match without spectators or, perhaps, a fire station without fires. It means nothing. Yes, 25th April is very near now and all we've been working for will be brought to nothing if we are not ready by then. Or, Sandy, if we look down on our customers.

Sandy: I know they're quite important Charles but sometimes I think it would be easier to run the museum without them.

Director: You may think that, Sandy. But it would mean running it without you too. Where would your salary come from Sandy? Now, I wanted to check with you today that all the plans we made two months ago are completed. And we want to see how you will behave when the public come in. Have you all brought with you things from your department – to talk about? Let's start with Eric. Now Eric, shoes. Remember what we said: shoe-making is a local industry and many people who come to the museum will know more about making shoes than any of us. Eric.

Eric: What has happened is that the old small shoe museum in the town centre has closed and we have taken over about half their exhibits – and added many others to them. Here is a typical boot, made for workmen. You'll see it has a large toe-end. That is because between the leather they used to put in a section of steel plate – to protect the toe against accident. I'll try it on. *(does so, with one boot)*. Now they are heavy but they are very safe – good for coal-mining, working on the roads, rail, etc.

Director: Eric, very good. I went down to your gallery when the museum was empty the other evening and it looked both complete but also very welcoming. I particularly like the 'hands-on' approach. And you have a shoe-maker there three times a week to help the public try their hands at cutting, stitching, etc. Very good. Let's try – Miriam.....

Miriam: Well, Charles, I think it was you that told me just how many famous sports people came from this area. And we have tried in our gallery to produce profiles on many of them. People like Frank Saunders who was voted the world's best rugby player back in 1897. We have a cut-out of him and lots of newspaper pieces about him – from local and national papers. The cut-out is very dramatic – he's leaping high to catch a ball in the line-out. 1899. We have about twenty famous people – from fishing to cross country running and from Ted Shack who virtually invented the pole vault to young Jamie Cross who only last year broke the world swimming record in his event. You'll see what we have done – made a replica of a swimming pool and we have a model of Jamie coming up to the finish. And we have computer machines which the public can use. They insert their tickets and see all the details, film, etc. about their chosen sports person. Their favourite.

Director: Excellent, Miriam. I hope you'll all have a chance to see Miriam's exhibition before we open on 25th.

Now, Sebastian. Can we hear from you, please?

Sebastian: Thanks, Charles. I am very happy to be connected with this new museum and new ways of running a museum. I'm sure it is all going to be very exciting.

Coins and medals are my business, as you know. And of course such things can look pretty dull when just set out on display. Except for the collectors, of course, who would go anywhere to study coins but who are only a small number. What to give the general public?

Well, we have tried two ideas to make the subject more interesting – user – friendly.

Each month we will feature different coins from different periods of history. We will have displays to show just what such coins could buy; how much people earned in a week; what the coins could buy in other countries.

Then we have made an arrangement with The Mint, in London, to have a show – three times a day – to show how coins are made today and how they were made in he past.

Director: Excellent. Now it is my pleasure to ask Magnus Donovan who has recently retired as Director of the National Museum, to talk to you – and to comment on what he has heard from Sandy, Miriam and Sebastian. Magnus – the floor is yours!

Magnus: It was very kind of Charles to invite me and I'm pleased to be here before you start. Often people ask me to comment when everything is settled and usually when it is all running. Too late!

You are certainly very lucky to have such a fine building for your project. Set in this beautiful park and yet close to the city centre.

Of course I know this fashion for new ideas of running a museum. But I have to say that what I have heard tells me that it is more like a theme park than anything I've experienced. You see to me a museum is for the person with an academic mind; someone who will study in depth; in silence. More for the specialist than the ordinary person.

Sandy: Sorry to disagree but the whole point of this museum is to change things. It is <u>for</u> the public. All of us want to get away from the fusty old buildings with everything behind glass; 'do not touch'.

Magnus: I was invited here to express my point of view.

Eric: Well, you know now that it is not our point of view. It is crazy in this day and age to take the money from the public and not let them see it, use it!

Director: Sorry, I'm going to interrupt. Jenny, would you please tell us about your gallery.

Jenny: Yes, Charles. I see my work as a direct link with education. We know from television how many people are interested today in archaeology. I hope to deepen their interest. We have set up three sites and the public can choose to either work on a site or watch others working. One site is of distant history and here – and, of course, keep this secret at all times – we have rocks bearing the fossils of dinosaurs. Those taking part have to read up some notes which give them clues about the time scale and there are more clues as they dig – pieces of bone, leaf fossils, etc. These are, of course, imitation but near enough. Anyone on this project must promise to give a whole day to join the team and they will be helped by students of archaeology. The other two sites are a grave of a Stone Age woman. And a Viking burial site.

Magnus: I'm sorry but this is madness. How can a person become an archaeologist within a day. It requires years of training. They are amateurs.

Jenny: Amateur means a lover of something, Mr Donovan!

(Silence – for several seconds. Tension)

Director: I think we should finish quite soon. I know you all have lots of work to do. Rather more than just putting things behind glass! Antony – can we hear, please?

Antony: Well, first of all, I would like to say how exciting the ideas are – especially Jenny's. Can I come and try the project out for you, Jenny?

My interest is what we call oral history. For many years you will know I have collected recordings on cassette and more recently on CD of older people talking about their memories of their youth; how it was in this area perhaps fifty, sixty years ago. But we don't want to stop this and those with longer lives will be asked to make perhaps a five minute recording – their memories of the war, the years of their young days. And we might ask them for their views of what has happened and how they find life today. Students of history from the local schools will be invited to join my staff and I, making the recordings. And we will build exhibits of photos and where possible of artefacts from their youth – for a future generation. Mr Heizner, whom you will know as a local dealer of art and bric-a-brac has promised to work with us in our collection. So - I see history as something continuing – not just stop and start.

Director: Thanks. Mrs Verity you have something special.

Mrs Verity: You all have heard of Fritz Hampner? He gave the world a very special way of making music. His widow has donated all his collection of musical instruments. Well, that is what he thought they were. Pots, pans, cans, chains, sticks – anything which would make a musical noise. He got his ideas from Africa where he lived for many years before retiring to this area. He also had a very special way of writing down the 'music' and we intend to let the public join us to do just that – make music. Charles has very kindly found us space well away from the rest of you!

Director: Well done, Mrs Verity. Well, that's all we have time for today. I'll be coming round to see your progress and I would like to thank you for getting me the brochure details 'on time'.

Oh, and thanks to Mr Donovan for his input. We hope we'll see you again, Magnus.

Scene 2

Director: It is only ten days since we met and now only two weeks before we open. And I'm afraid I have some bad news. I'll ask Adrian, our financial director, to tell you. Adrian.

Adrian: You all know that to start our project we were dependent on our Culture Committee to start us off. They had promised to finance this 'museum'. You also know that in the recent election we had a change of party and I'm afraid they have sent me a letter saying that we have dropped down their list of priorities and we will receive only 75% of the money we were promised. Somehow we must make cuts in our spending. The worst thing would be for us to end our first year with a loss – a large loss.

Director:	You should know that the Culture Committee took advice from Magnus Donovan. I should never have invited him to join us. This is my fault but I was just trying to be open.
Sandy:	What can we do?
Jenny:	Charles, we can't blame you. It seems to me that we can either close for three months a year. Not open on, say, Mondays and Tuesday. Lose yourself or Adrian. Maybe we could close down a department… What does anyone think? *(Fades)*

A further scene could be written by two fast-track students, using some local idea; perhaps from their own area.

The whole play could develop to be the working museum with those playing the parts here in charge of running a section – possibly with another class as 'the public'. You could create a 'Magnus' type museum where the public is bored and the helpers actually half-asleep!

Let Magnus be played by the teacher……?

See Projects – Museum (p. 117)

'CLOAK DARROW FARM'

CAST:

Vanda	(Group Leader)
Sonda	(Manager)
Louka	(Member)
Toller	(Member)
Gloose	(Member)
Palieri	(Member)
Anda	(Member)
Pollo	(Member)
Gilkes	(Member)

Recorded voice(s)

Sonda: Where is Pollo? Has anyone seen her?

All: No. She was missing yesterday. She phoned me last night and seemed OK. Haven't seen her since the last meeting.

Sonda: Well, we've got to get on. Password, please.

(They go in turn to Sonda and whisper a password. Then go back to their seats. Palieri can't remember his password)

Palieri – you had better think fast. We only changed it last week – after the affair with that traitor Parma. You know what happened to him?

Palieri: Sorry, Sonda. *(He tries again – successfully)*

Sonda: Lucky you. By the way, it isn't funny. We must be sure that no-one, absolutely no-one from 'outside' knows anything of this – anything. Be sure of that.

	Now you have all heard from Vanda since we last met. Today we must go over the details. I don't need to say that each of our lives depends on each other. One slip and we all could fail. But first a word from our leader. Vanda....
Vanda:	'Cloak Darrow'. Friends. We meet not only for ourselves but for the whole community. The Parma affair we have put behind us. He was a big mistake. He threatened our very lives. He was the rotten apple in our barrel. Be warned about him. That is all I want to say –
Pollo:	*(Rushes in – breathless)* Sorry Vanda. I left my papers behind and had to go back to collect them.
Sonda:	Pollo – see me after we have finished this meeting. Take your seat – and quickly. Please finish, Vanda.
Vanda:	Pollo – see me too. Now Sonda, let's get down to the serious business. All stand. Repeat after me:

"I am part of a team with a serious purpose. The cause is to eliminate a danger to our society. In this I pledge my very life to the cause".

(Vanda repeats this a sentence at a time and the others repeat it after him)
Now, please be seated. Sonda.... |
| **Sonda:** | The main idea of this meeting is to check that you have completed the work you were given. And that you know exactly what the others are doing. Firstly, Louka. Please feel free to make notes. |
| **Louka:** | We have finished the survey. With the help of a helicopter we now have an accurate picture of the building. Our thermal imaging camera has shown which rooms are in use. |

We have also surveyed the grounds of the farm and my assistant has found an entrance which seems free of cameras, guard dogs, etc. Here are some papers which you should study.

(They look at Louka's papers, discuss them)

Sonda: Next, Toller. Please.

Toller: 'Cloak Darrow'. I was given the job of checking on all communications. I now have a full picture of the farm and how it is wired – telephone, cables, dishes, etc. With my team we have made a plan how to isolate the farm and disconnect all these systems. And we have the Interferon machine which can make sure that all radio signals are blocked and made useless.

Sonda: Well done, Toller. Any questions?

Anda: How long before we go in will you cut all these communications?

Toller: At minus 15 all communications to the farm will cease. We will set up a controlled explosion at the electrical station to make it look as if this was the cause of the cut-off. You can see that at point 6F on Louka's plan 3.

Sonda: Good. And Anda, you…..

Anda: I have hired three experts all of whom have been trained in 'termination'. They won't know <u>why</u> they are doing this but they do know <u>what</u> to do and will complete their task exactly to plan. They will be using the new gas technique which, as you know, knocks out anyone who might get in our way. This we will also use on our target, as you know we intend to bring him out alive and to be tried by a people's court. Palieri…

Palieri: I take over from Anda. As the target is carried out we will have a vehicle waiting next to the entrance we are using. This then drives for just three minutes to the field where the helicopter waits.

Sonda: That's better, Palieri. Next meeting we hope to hear more from you about those last minutes – what happens if you find doors locked, any other emergencies. Lastly, Gloose……

Gloose: The masks are almost finished. They are easy to wear and no-one will even know your sex, your gender when you are masked. As there is to be no violence, at any stage, the masks are your best protection. Denner had the masks made *(and here are some examples for you to try on)*

Sonda: Lastly, Pollo. How about transport?

Pollo: You all know that my team will be stealing a car – a BMW – on the afternoon of the 17th. We will re-spray the car in Rostu's garage and that is all arranged.. But Sonda I'm having some trouble getting a helicopter – well not the machine but the pilot. The guy wants to charge 10K.

Sonda: This is crazy. We should have known about this weeks ago. Vanda, How about the money?

Vanda: The helicopter is an essential part of our plan. Without it we could never get the target away – it's obvious. The money will be found. Pollo – go ahead with your plans. Ring me at home when they're completed. Sonda…..

Sonda: Well, it was all going well. Thank you. But I'm worried about the helicopter. Surely you could find another pilot, another company?

Pollo: There are very few people who would take the risk, Sonda. We are paying for the risk.

Sonda: Are there any more questions – from any of you? This is certainly our last meeting. Don't forget we rendezvous at 10.00pm on ------

Gilkes: *(Rushing in)* ….. 'Cloak Darrow'. Sonda – a real emergency. Listen to this *(produces cassette player/radio)*

Recorded Voice: "…on the European front. In Parliament it was announced that a plot had been discovered to kidnap Mr L – the pseudonym used by a member of the Foreign Office with special powers of negotiation in the Government's new Peace Initiative. A government spokesman made these comments:

(At this point a new voice makes a statement about information which has just come into the Government's hands. Added to the cassette message)

(Silence)

Sonda: Please remain seated. Security – lock the doors. No-one leaves. I wish to have a few words with Vanda. At this moment in time everyone is a suspect. Stay in your seats……

'OUT OF THE CUBE'

a short play with 10 opportunities for improvisation

CAST:

Tomas:	A	A sympathetic young guard, conscripted
Lenta:	B	A hardened guard, woman
Zef:	C	A third guard
Josephine:	D	A young freedom-fighter or terrorist, girl of 14+
Eva:	E	Her mother
Franz:	F	Her brother
Father Pau:	G	Their Priest

(NB: Sections underlined are subject to improvisation by the group – <u>as long as</u> they realise what follows in the narrative).

A: *(reading a newspaper).* Here we are. To buy – or to borrow? To sell – or to lend? 'A room in a quiet part of town. Simple but effective. All meals provided – breakfast, luncheon, tea and dinner. Sunny aspect. Free!' Whew!!! *(to audience)* Oh, you thought I was reading the paper. No it's here I mean. This place. No <u>not</u> the stage but this little box inside the stage. Here. 'A quiet room, Simple. Meals thrown in. Sun. And free!' And me!!

My name is Tomas. This is my place. I look after it and it looks after me. Just for now. I call it The Cube. I think someone's coming – another of the president's guests, a customer, client – nice words those. Did you notice, I like words. I'm trying to learn English. This – job – is all I could get. I am here because the community sent me here. They said: "Go to Sandry Prison –

until the schools and colleges are open again" And do you know, I agreed! You have to agree. I'll just give it a little clean …… freshen it up for the customer ….. the President's guest! Quite easy this bit *(he cleans 'it' – a bench, a slop bucket, the door grill.)*

B: My little box of tricks. Too good for some of them. Too big. Tomas is on guard today. I come on guard at 6.00 this evening. Look at it – the cheapest hotel in town. They pay nothing, do nothing, say very little. Useless to us all. The fools who want to change everything. Some of them are just twelve years old – some younger. You'll see. What can they change? Why change? The country isn't perfect <u>but</u> – the country isn't fair <u>but</u> – the country isn't free <u>but</u> – you know the 'buts'…… It's worse in many other places; it could be worse with them, who knows? You know what I would do with the little beggars?…..

(B goes)

A: There we are. All nice for the guests. My little box. I call it 'the Cube' but you know a cube has got an outside and this has only got an inside – that's what the last guest said. And he should know – he was in it for ten years, poor devil.

Oh, someone's coming. A quick tidy……. Paper away….. Attention!

C: Here it is, Tomas.

A: Sir!

C: Well, open up then. Put her in. She can cool off in there. Plenty of time to think about it. In you go *(D, a girl of 14 or more, is bundled into the cell)* Well, Tomas, a full house again. How's it going, lad?

A: It's going, sir.

C: Now, about this one. No feeding the animals for about 24 hours. They proved they can be tough, now we'll see if they can be weak. A bowl of water. And a blanket. That's all my dog gets.

A: It's a girl, sir.

C: No matter. She doesn't act like one. Water, blanket – alright?

A: What's it like out there, sir?

C: Not very easy. Since the announcement was made, they've taken to the streets. The army has been sent in. The police can't cope.

A: So, it's the army tanks against the kids with stones is it?

C: That's the front line. What lies behind it?

I'd better get back. Now remember. No softness. No sympathy. No mercy. We'll soften her up. Even if she is only 14. *(He goes)*

(A goes in another direction for water and blanket; D produces a small radio from somewhere and turns it on, after checking the guard's absence. We hear a jumbled signal on an ancient radio. <u>Work out what it might say</u> ....

D removes radio and hides it as A returns)

A: *(Opens door and takes in water bowl and blanket. Exchanges looks with D)*

It's girls now, is it? *(D doesn't answer any question).* You against the army? Should be in school – oh, no – there's no school. Forgot! Mother know you are here? That's all I'm allowed to give you. Now don't do anything silly or I'll be the next one inside – The Cube. OK? Give me a call, if you need anything – I'm down the corridor. OK? *(He goes. She arranges the bedroll. Inspects some bruises. Lies back and then – slowly produces the radio and listens with it close to her ear)* Scene fades...

Scene 2

A: *(Opening cell door)* Come on, wakey, wakey! Stand by your bed. Well, say something. I bet you're not so dumb out there, on the streets. Look here - I understand *(whispers)* Did it myself once. You can tell me. How did you get involved?

D: No.

A: Look young lady, I was in to it once – not so long ago. I do understand – I even sympathise. *(in whisper)*

D: How do you know? How do you know anything? Working here. In this place?

A: If you must know – I was sent here too.

D: Then let me out. Let me get back to the others. If you mean it.

A: Now listen, miss: I might agree with everything – I'm not saying. But I'd be a fool to let you out. I would be in more trouble than you. They're not playing games, you know. Have to look after myself – and that means looking after you.

D: Coward!

A: Maybe I am. But I've got my own skin to look after. Now you cool down *(telephone rings in distance)*. Oh, there's the 'phone. Now you stay just there. I'll be back later. Don't try anything silly now. *(He exits to 'phone). (The girl sits on the 'bed'. Tries radio but batteries seem to have given out. She listens at wall. Rubs bruised arms and legs. Sits with water bowl on lap – waiting for his return)*

A: Now, where were we? Oh, yes, the phone. That was the boss ringing from Central Police. Your mother went there and they told her you were here. She's coming down. You are allowed five minutes only. And you are lucky. They don't usually see many visitors here *(Fade)*

Scene 3

(Mother brought to cell door by A)

E: D, what have they got you here for?

D: I was picked up in Cosmo Street. *(Mother and daughter, <u>continues conversation</u>. A has locked them in the cell. He signs off and departs).*

(After 3 minutes B appears).

B: Come on you. Out! Get out!!

Five minutes, eh. You've been here for at least fifteen. Out. Or you can spend the night here too – with a blanket between you.

E: Alright, I will!

B: Now look here; I don't want any trouble from you. There's quite enough with her here. I thank God she's no daughter of mine. A disgrace. That's what she is. A disgrace to the country. She should be helping at home instead of playing the hero on the streets. You should be ashamed of her. Now get out!

(E exits)

Mother? She doesn't deserve the title 'mother'. Bringing you into the world. Bringing you up. To throw stones at the police. Set fire to cars and buses. Paint stupid slogans on the walls. If I had my way *(B comes across and grabs D by the hair but looks towards the door and releases her with contempt)* – ergh!!!

B: Why don't you rush for the door – then I could do my job properly. *(B exits, locking door. D rearranges hair and peers out of door grill as light fades)*

Scene 4

A: Here we are *(opening cell)* Not much but it's what you're allowed – plus a little egg of my own. Now, for God's sake eat it down – I told you what they'd do to me. Now here's a mystery parcel. Keep it down and don't forget to give it back to me before I go off tonight. If B sees or hears it she'll take great pleasure in shopping me. *(Leaves package with transistor in it)* Now what did your mum say? Nice to see here, I suppose.

D: Yes. Thanks for the radio. I'll listen quietly. Oh, mother. You can imagine what she said. *(<u>Repeats conversation</u> she had with mother)*

A: Well, I must go. It's getting worse out there. They sent a force over from Dilar. You were safest in here last night, I tell you. I'll be back later. Now cheer up. I'm on duty this week in the days. And you can sleep in the nights. OK?

(D sees him off. Smartens up herself and her bedroll. And very carefully takes out the transistor and tunes in. We hear some music and the announcer breaks in with <u>message</u>. D listens carefully. And turns set off and breaks down in tears on the bed. Like the little girl that she is)

Scene 5

D: Who's there?

A: A surprise.

F: It's me, D.

A: In you go. You've got five minutes – officially!

F: Hello. D – what a place.

D: Franz! What are you doing here?

F: Mother sent me.

D: Yes, she was here.

F: I thought you should know how it's going?

D: I've heard some bad news. A. smuggled in a radio and I have been listening to it, from time to time. It sounds bad.

F: Yes. The group from Tamley tried to get through to join us but the army just took them out. There are several dead and many arrested outside the town. By the way – are you bugged?

D: I don't know but you must tell me – where are Senca and Grill?

(F <u>explains</u>. *And the scene fades*).

Scene 6

B: This way, your reverence. The girl is under punishment and you have five minutes. Not a moment more.

G: D!

D: Father Pau. Another visitor. Bringing the world into my box. 'The Cube', as A. calls it.

G: How are they treating you? That one looks frightening.

D: A. is OK. and <u>she</u> B is what she looks. Sold out to the party. Enjoying her power.

G: The Cube, eh? I was always told that a cube was a strong shape. This is a mean looking place. What has been happening to you? *(D tells the story) of her arrest; her mother's visit; her brother's news, etc.).*

D: Tell me about the state of things – out there on the streets. Is it working?

G: D, if I told you that I would be in some danger myself – you know *(looks heavenwards)*. How <u>can</u> I tell you? When you were there we had perhaps twenty thousand people involved. A network of groups. We had charge of the transport – or most of it. And the power supply. The university was 100% with us. And there were groups of grown-ups at every point. They had even arranged a mass protest for tomorrow. BUT: *(explains what has happened)* They brought their great monsters in and crushed everyone, everything…… there are tanks everywhere, soldiers at every corner, the police visiting houses. No-one trusts anyone with the ADZ around. We are left with a handful of fanatics, throwing stones at ¼ inch armour and trying to lift the cobbles with torn fingers. Only your name is there to remind us how near we got – 'D'…….. *(fades)*

Scene 7

D: *(lying on her bed……. listens to the radio <u>Bulletin</u>.)*

B: Stand up. Now, where did you find – that *(indicating radio)*?

How did that get in here? Mother, brother, priest – eh? I'll have that – although you've probably heard the news. Too late now, isn't it? Now: continue our little conversation – remember what I said: if you don't tell me everything you'll be immediately handed over to Garcia – and you know what his reputation is – with prisoners.

D: I told you…… I've told you everything.

(she looks out, <u>telling the story</u> as if to herself)

…… and when my father died, there was no-one to take over….

No-one to lead…. Everyone had looked to my father….. he was a good man…… a great man. Everything he did was for his people. Not for some great giant of a system but for everyone's good – yours, A's, yes, even Garcia's if he did but know it. I had joined the Halling Commando as a small child….. running messages….. I learnt to know every corner of the city…..when to appear….. how to look innocent. Often the police would let me through – or clip my ears as a beggar –

B: What were the names of the others? Come on!

D: They are certainly dead, from what I heard on the news. So you will never know that. You'll have to kill me to find out. Remember father, there is lots of him just in here…. *(A. rushes in, with a note)*

B: *(<u>Reads the note</u>)* So, my friends. It is all over. The party has just announced that. The last few have either surrendered of 'gone to ground'. We'll find them. The ADZ group are good at that game – a big cat and some very small mice! It's over. Another revolution over and –

(D rushes for B but suddenly turns sideways. Grabs A's gun. Backs into a corner).

D: I only need one shot just now. The first gun I've handled but father showed me how. *(She aims gun at B)* To Father – Halling Commando – and the people *(Turns gun suddenly on self and fires)*

B: The stupid fool. She didn't wait.

A: What do you mean, wait.

B: The end of the message. The instructions were to let her go. The committee thought she was no threat….. a teenage leader of what?….. A 14 year old general with no army? And her value in keeping the mass quiet was outside.

A: So 'The Cube' has an outside.

B: Yes.

A: And you and I have got to live on the outside. I'll tell you something B, she's better off where she is – that's what I think and what I think she thinks.

B: What about this radio, A? How did that get in here. Most careless of you. Could have been bad for you – if there had been an inspection, you know.

A: Must have been the priest – or the mother *(they drift away)* perhaps.

B Well, that one solved itself. Garcia might even give you promotion…. *(as they leave)* See to the body.

THE PROJECTS

PROJECT

'Sculptures'

This short project can be delivered within the length of a school lesson. It will take longer – perhaps a second lesson – if one sees developments in the idea and it is working well.

The group should be divided into threes. Name themselves A, B and C. Then, the task: In each group A is to represent a master sculptor. An individual whose work is priceless and who shows in the world's leading galleries. B is his apprentice. C represents the raw material which this workshop uses, be it clay, wood, plastic etc.

There is one simple but necessary instruction. A is the teacher but must **not** touch the sculpture him/herself. B fashions the sculpture according to A's teaching advice. C is inanimate and, like all good raw material, allows itself to be sculpted!

A good floor space is necessary. A teaches, B works and C does nothing. Perhaps 15 minutes is needed to fashion the various pieces – perhaps 8 or 10 sets in a normal class. The teacher can advise A and B to make the piece bold but balanced, as poor C will have to remain in situ for some time. Of course B has to manipulate the raw material and should be advised to seek detail, not just a general shape. For instance, the eyes, mouth and tilt of the head are vital elements in this work of art.

Once the sculpture is complete the teacher invites A and B to (a) give the piece a title, suitable for a catalogue and (b) suggest a sale price. All the processes thus far should demand speech and listening skills, between A and B.

The teacher now declares that the various pieces are to be exhibited and sold in a gallery. B stands on duty with his/her creation while the A characters go shopping, round the galleries. Each B has to explain the piece, its value, name, price. They can barter over the price. Discuss the article, ask if other copies could be made, find if the piece would weather well in an outdoor setting. Eventually (perhaps 15 minutes) the As and the Bs agree, on price, transport, background, etc. Or they disagree!

At this point the teacher can adopt the role of a wealthy art-lover who decides to outbid everyone else. He/she says the pieces are to be taken, with due and great care, to the docks where a small circle denotes the amount of space for all the pieces being shipped across the Atlantic. As and Bs (perhaps with help from each other) bring their priceless artefacts to the docks knowing that any breakages will cancel the order. They work together to get the pieces into the smallest space, ready for export. With T.L.C.!

The developments and variations in these exercises should and do emerge organically from the work put into them. Both student and teacher can easily find ways to extend an activity without losing its essence. Indeed, an imaginative response is built into the style of work. Time might prove to be the major restriction. With 'Sculptures' it will be obvious that the parts of A, B and C can be rotated. This always ensures that poor C has a chance for revenge or that A and B are careful to make their demands practicable!

The project might work if there are four in each group, with two Bs. Here, in language terms, A will have two people to instruct. Of course you can have two Cs, ensuring a more composite sculpture, allowing more contrasts, perhaps.

An advanced group might decide to let C show some awkwardness or difficulty in complying. I'm sure it is obvious that B has to physically 'construct' the sculpture and as C has no voice (or ears) it can't be simply told to do things for itself. C has to realise that the task has to be completed – whether awkward or not.

An almost balletic response is for C to take on more human characteristics while it is possible that A and B can 'catch' the problem and finish up more robotic than C.

Some of these ideas might take this exercise in the direction of 'presentation' but in its original form it is clearly intended more for process than product.

PROJECT

'The Village'

This project is based upon the students' own community, be it village, town or city. It could be worked using an imaginary place or a mixture.

To begin with a set of slides is required and a projector for them. These slides could be taken by an older group – perhaps as a media project. They need to be well shot, with an imaginative set of buildings and features from the locality.

Perhaps a set of 30 slides is needed. They should be of places such as:

> The Church
> A housing estate – private and community
> The local aerodrome
> The swimming pool
> The shop
> The cemetery
> Old people's home
> The village/town hall
> A farm
> A riding stable
> The cricket ground etc. etc.

Once the slides are processed the teacher (or indeed the photographers) must write a paragraph about each place from the point of view of the person who inhabits or works there. The writer should avoid 'naming' the profession of the person; and avoid naming the actual building or place. Thus:

> 'I work here about 10 hours a week and I used to work in the old building which wasn't so easy. We built this new place with some money from the Lottery. It is used several times each week. I have to do most clearing up on Sundays – after the football club has used the changing rooms'.

So each slide has a matching written card. The cards need to be typed and laminated as they will be used by many different hands. The preparations are now ready for the activity to proceed.

Now the teacher gives each student a map of the locality, with each feature marked on the map. It helps to have a north pointer and some notion of scale.

In Stage 1 the slides and cards are placed at random on a large table which should be in an 'island' situation – so that every student can walk round it. The projector can be set up nearby.

The students are asked to match up each slide with its appropriate card – the place with the person. For the first ten minutes this can be a slow process but eventually as mix-and-match takes place students take a slide and card with them and find a seat, leaving more space and fewer options for the remainder. Eventually (perhaps with some guidance from the teacher) each person has a slide and its correct card. They take them to their seats, read them and start to take on the character and his/her situation.

For Stage 2 the teacher should have invited two guests to come to the classroom. Perhaps the headmaster and secretary; perhaps strangers from outside the school. It could be a caretaker and his wife!

The teacher has briefed these visitors thus: they are thinking of moving to the village, town, etc. They need information about life there. There are experts around to explain the place to them! Stage 1 will probably take half an hour and slightly more than ten minutes is needed for the visitors to make their enquiries. It may be best to use two lessons – one one week and the Stage 2 the following week.

The students are warned that visitors are expected. They prepare themselves to answer any queries. Before the visitors appear the students get their slides together in some order in the magazine. They should be listed so that they can be found quickly, for the visitors to see. The visitors are given a list of the places and find reasons to ask about them. Thus:

"Our son in a very keen swimmer. Are there any facilities for swimming here?"

"What shopping facilities are there, locally?"

"We want our aged mother to live near us. Is there an old people's home? What is it like?"

The students take on their character and answers the visitors' questions. Possibly going beyond the facts written on their card.

It is usual for the students to try to 'sell' the community to the newcomers but it is possible to run this whole project where they consciously try to put the visitors off, making it sound as unattractive as possible. A further development is that every student is a friend and even relation of everyone else. They can recommend each other – or perhaps warn the visitors.

An intelligent class could make this work develop from a geography or civics lesson. It might be possible for it to develop into an input to school assembly – for others to watch; and perhaps join in.

PROJECT

'Creating a Character'

A play is clearly a balance between its characters and its plot. In this activity we stress the building of a character. Of course, such a character could be part of a novel and even perhaps a poem.

A very fruitful development of drama and theatre involved the stereotypical characters of the Commedia del Arte. In this project it might be best to work against stereotype and to give maximum individuality to all the characters invented. It might be possible for them to meet up and interact; again in a stereotypical situation where people are 'thrust together' such as a broken-down lift, a desert island or a doctor's waiting room. Bringing a set of disparate characters together can be the culmination of this work – what on earth could they have in common!

Organise the group or class in threes. In each trio ask one to be scribe. This job can rotate as the project develops. Ideally the work can proceed over perhaps ten weeks, ten lessons. This gives time for the process to deepen and for work to be done between class sessions.

Each group is then asked to 'create a character', a person from the present, past, even future. A golden rule is that all three <u>must</u> agree on every stage of their character. If there is disagreement invite the sub-group to start again. Perhaps twenty minutes is needed for the first draft, for negotiation between the threesome, and for the recording progress. After this first attempt the teacher asks the group to introduce its new 'character' to the other sub-groups. This is the foundation on which the remaining work is built.

Some groups will begin with a name, perhaps an address. Others may begin with some characteristic such as 'she is 74 years old and only has one leg'. Once they have heard each other, give the groups some further time to broaden their character – picking up points they have heard from the others.

So far each group should have created a fairly rounded character about whom we know something. The sub-group usually begins to 'own' the character at this time.

Next, the teacher asks the groups to work strictly as individuals and gives them a quiz. They don't compare notes at this stage. The following type of questions are asked and each replies in the spirit of their character:

1. What newspaper would the person take?
2. What pet might the character keep?
3. Does the person ever bet, gamble?
4. How does the character view 'sex' – scoring 1 for 'low interest' to 5 'high interest'.
5. What social class does the person belong to?
6. Where would the person spend their dream holiday?
7. How do they view regulation?
8. Who is the person's next-of-kin?
9. Would you call them 'introvert' or 'extrovert'?
10. How would the person vote?
11. Who would the character like to have been; their hero?

When completed the teacher allows the sub-groups to re-form and compare notes, seeing if there is any correlation or agreement between them. These results can be discussed when high levels of agreement might suggest stereotyping; disagreement suggesting individuality or a part-formed character. This phase of the activity probably sets the seal on subsequent success in the building of the character.

The next phase gives the sub-group time to 'tidy up' their character. It might be appropriate here to let the group choose who from perhaps the acting world they would cast and, more complex, who amongst the whole class they would choose to play the part – assuming this was all there was.

With a 'person' now developing the teacher can invite each sub-group to put their person into a situation. Possibly a day in their life when something momentous happened to them be it sad or happy, character-making. In this respect it might be necessary to allow the sub-group to invent the 'meaningful others' in their lives: family, workmates, partner, children. In each threesome one could play the character and the other two get involved with their life, with their dominant moment.

By now some five weeks may have elapsed and the person has moved from outline to detailed. The group can be asked to do a drawing of their character and a representation of their home. These can be presented to the other sub-groups.

The sub-group now work together on writing an epitaph or obituary on their character – not that they are dead (yet).

In Irwin Shaw's book 'The Young Lions' three characters are followed in alternate chapters. The reader may experience some difficulty knowing how this will develop and for Shaw the three characters are all somehow involved in each others death, on a wartime battlefield. This idea can be used with the teacher trying to match up two or three characters who somehow impinge on each others life. A plot develops and we are moving the characters into a play in which they are mutually interactive.

No doubt the students can begin to build in extra aspects, if there is time. Once they 'own' the character they will suggest ideas for development.

A suitable ending is that each character receives a letter from a local lawyer. These letters can be tailor-made to provide some dilemma for a particular character. Thus for a bachelor the condition of benefiting from a Will is that the character must be married before; or that someone can't inherit until they have accomplished some stated task. However this is not mentioned in the letter. The lawyer requests the character to attend his office and only then reveals the condition for inheritance. Here one of the sub-group can play the lawyer and one the character and the third his/her friend. This visit to the lawyer and negotiation over the terms of the Will (left by a distant relative) can form the climax of this particular project.

At each stage of character-building the students can observe each others work. The teacher will decide in consultation with the various groups if they wish to do this and also if time allows.

'creating a character'

Check list – ten stages

1. Meet in threes. Appoint scribe
   First discussion together

2. Report back. Broaden the character

3. Individual quiz re character; compare notes

4. Further broadening – social class, education, etc.

5. Place character in important situation and 'meaningful others' e.g. next-of-kin

6. Character's home; appearance

7. Who would play character – actor and member of trio

8. Character's epitaph, obituary

9. Meeting between characters invented

10. Summoned by lawyer

Other possible tasks: make out character's school report.

Find out character's 'hero'

Create a network of those most significant in character's life, etc. etc.

Example of two meetings:

Louise Carstairs is a woman in 'reduced circumstances'.
In her later years she has taken up an interest in archaeology. She is a spinster of 58, living in Sussex.

Her life reaches its high point when she attends the Summer School (in archaeology) at her local university. She is attending this summer school and has been at the last night party – before returning to her comfortable yet lonely home a few miles away. She has an unfulfilled emotional life and fears being on her own. She craves for…….

Germain de Trusse. He died several hundred years ago whilst accompanying William the Conqueror. He was killed by a stray arrow and buried where he lay. He has a family in Col de Grêve, including three young children. He is in a reserve army of the Conqueror and expected to return home after perhaps six months.

Germain is a farmer. But he is also an inventor very interested in alchemy. He is also fascinated by the past but never expected to be involved in an archaeological dig in the Sussex countryside – for his own body. Louise is the first person to see him for 900 years…….

Or

Peter Lacrovic is a twelve year old boy. He is an orphan living in a care home in Southern England.

Peter attends the local school where he receives special help with his English. He comes from Kosovo where his parents were killed in fighting six years ago. He has an English sponsor family called Peterson but they live in Scotland.

Peter seems to have a natural ability in music and he plays the piano brilliantly. The care home warden is looking for sponsorship so that he can be properly trained……

Jens Palme-Nielsen is a Dane, living in England. He is a bachelor of 73 who has made his fortune in shipping. He is told by his doctors that he has a progressive illness which cannot be reversed.

Jens has no-one to leave his money to. The last of his family in Denmark have died and they were never close to him. His closest friend is an English headmaster – his former tennis partner. He happens to be Head of the school where some refugees attend……

PROJECT

'The Martians'

This project at present lies in the area of fantasy much as radio did in 1850 and The Genome did in 1950. As this writer predicts it as a normal idea for 2050 we had best be prepared. As this writer predicts he will be a long way away by 2050 – it doesn't really matter. But our imagination does!

How would we explain ourselves to visitors from outer space: our customs, behaviour, life style? Remember <u>we</u> are in outer space to them.

In this project we can develop to its fullest the idea of the Information Gap. While the group is dividing itself into, say, eight sub groups of 3s or 4s the teacher quietly withdraws one group composed of the 3 or 4 of the brightest or the quickest. This group (yes, soon to be, Martians) meet apart and are unannounced. More on them later.

Those remaining join ranks for a brainstorming session. What activities do we humans do? These should be listed and the following list will emerge, hopefully with minimum direction from the teacher:

    We   build homes
               work
               live together – produce young
               die
               are ill
               have hobbies – sports etc.
               watch TV
               take holidays
               gain an education
               cook; feed
               fight each other
               sleep
               have Gods etc.

Each sub-group chooses one from this list. They then work up a short scene depicting the action of, say, a typical family meal, a day in the life of a school, packing for a holiday.

They are encouraged to 'polish' their idea and perhaps be lightly warned that 'someone else may be interested in what you're doing'.

Meanwhile the teacher can be working elsewhere with the single group. These are the Martians. They are friendly, <u>very</u> curious and happen to speak English! Soon they will visit earth and meet its inhabitants. They wish to co-operate but may not know what a meal is or why it seems to enter the mouth. The Martians can wear half-masks. These allow them to speak while quickly making them look different.

When everything seems ready the teacher leads the Martians to the earth people and becomes the link between them. Of course the earth groups entertain their guests but verbal explanations may not be enough. Would the Martians enjoy trying a breakfast, attending a school, seeing a house being built? The Martians are led around the various groups and the other earth people can circulate with them as spectators.

Eventually the Martians must depart. They say their goodbyes, make a few comments about earth-life and perhaps take a few sample earth-people with them.

(The scene is in a school – a typical class lesson)

Martian 1:	What are you doing?
Student:	This is a class – at school
M1:	Sorry – what is that word 'class' – and what means 'school'?
Student:	Oh sorry. Well school is the thing you go to when you are young. You have to learn in school. Learn to read, to count – everything really.
M1:	We know 'learn'. But we 'learn' with a new computer programme which Gargo makes for us.
Student:	Gargo?
M1:	Yes. He is our leader and he knows very much. Why are you together in 'school'?
Student:	I don't know, really. Maybe it is cheaper to teach so many together.

Student 2:   Because we also learn about each other – and about life. And its fun.

M2:   There *is* only one life.

Student 1:   But human life ends – at about 80.

M1:   Ends?

Etc.

The 'Martian' activity can, of course, focus on specific aspects of life rather than the general list suggested here. Thus the emphasis could be on (human) sports with the locals using examples such as:

> football
> skiing
> judo
> tennis
> chess
> and cricket (difficult to explain to another human!)

The house and the workplace could have similar treatment to this. Also 'crime and punishment'; 'marriage'; 'multi-culturism', etc. could be tackled.

Cross-refer to the play 'Visitors'.

PROJECT

'The Balloon'

The balloon debate is a very familiar project and of itself hardly needs inclusion here. But on this occasion I have added a dimension to it by writing some poems which could be used by those taking part.

For those unfamiliar with it the basic idea concerns a society which is in peril. The country has to be evacuated and, for the future good, it is best that those most useful to mankind are saved – presumably to help form a new society elsewhere. A balloon is available and there are about ten places in the basket of the balloon. The students can help decide which professions are to be included and then each chooses one of these. They then have to argue for the inclusion of their 'character' in the balloon. Justify his place. Unfortunately once the balloon takes off it is found to be too heavy (or the gas runs out!) and each 'character' has to make an argument as to why they should stay on board. The balloon must be lighter. A vote is taken and the loser on each occasion has to be ditched overboard. Time must be given for the passengers to prepare their case which they must argue strenuously.

Round by round they argue for their survival, as a character essential for the future of the species. If time is scarce, perhaps two characters can be thrown out of the balloon each round. Eventually, with its lighter load, the balloon continues to its destination.

The following are often chosen to begin the first round:

- Priest
- Teacher
- Farmer
- Poet/Artist
- Politician
- Lawyer
- Inventor
- Doctor
- Soldier
- Philosopher

But other ideas can be added such as a pregnant woman, or a child, a scientist.

Each character is given perhaps five minutes to present the case for his/her survival. Of course if a character survives the first round he or she will have to argue again in round two.

And onwards. As the project develops it is likely that, say, the priest may question the right of perhaps the teacher or the lawyer to progress; as much to eliminate others as to establish one's own place in the Balloon. At each round it is probably practicable to give each speaker one minute less to make their case. In a large group of course two students can work together representing one profession, expressing different aspects of the same argument. It is clearly a serious exercise in essence. Although it often plays with humour.

The balloon debate can be built around famous historical characters such as: Nelson Mandela, Michael Faraday, Florence Nightingale, Winston Churchill, Adolf Hitler, Alexander the Great, Jesus, etc.

The following verses may help certain 'characters':

'PRIEST'

I'm halfway up to heaven
And close in touch with God
Just catch a view of paradise
Far from our earthly sod.

    My job is fighting evil
    In prayer, down on my knees,
    Outwitting of the Devil
    In search for love and peace.

The sign of hope – the steeple
Follow the Master's light
And help all kinds of people
To fight their endless fight.

    If this seems paradoxic
    To fight a war for peace
    Let's call it theosophic
    And get down on our knees.

My job contains a mystery
To die and rise again
But all the church's history
Links pleasure up with pain.

    If you can't understand this
    Let me see if I can
    Because I'm nicely placed here
    Halfway twixt God and Man!

'THE TEACHER'

The species 'common teacher'
You really can't reject,
From pupil, parent, public
He emanates respect

In the past the wealthy
Education could command,
This proved not very healthy
So hence the new demand.

A future generation
Will really need his skills
A decent education
Protects against all ills

A parent is a teacher,
A manager the same.
This is the common feature
We all must play the game

The 'game' of course, is 'living'
The teacher sets the tone
The world seems unforgiving
For those who go alone.

'FARMER'

I plough the fields and scatter
The embryonic seed
For it must really matter
The kind of food we feed.

My cows and sheep and pigs are
Your beef and lamb and pork
These keep your healthy figure
Of which we always talk.

The milk shed and the tractor
The earth, the rain, the sun,
These are the common factors
From which my work is spun.

All people need a farmer
Just simply to survive
And Nature, do not harm her
If we're to stay alive.

I work on that mosaic
Of pasture, meadow, fields
Both sacred and prosaic
The crops the farmer yields.

All flora and all fauna
Help farmers to exist
And life would be much poorer
If our kind don't exist.

'THE ARTIST'

Is there space for an artist on your journey?
Can I justify my place in your balloon?
While I spend my life creating
Perhaps below there's someone waiting
Who really should have taken up, have taken up this precious room?

What do I add
To the sum of human happiness?
Happy or sad
My life's a different way.
How can I feel
If I am good or valueless,
Imaginary or real:
Who is prepared to say?

Then listen to my words:
Perhaps a simple melody,
Sounds you never heard
Sung quite this way before;
Colour and design
In chaos or in harmony,
Caught in space and time
We touched and heard and saw.

The drama of our dreams
So distant from reality;
Not always as it seems,
The workings of our mind.
Beneath the human mask
Creative human quality
The artist has to ask
And find what he can find.

A vision of the world
In song and word and motion,
A banner we've unfurled
To show mankind's unique.
Our innermost resources
Deepest held emotion
Life's creative forces
Are what the artists seek.

'THE POLITICIAN'

If ever you a politician see,
You'll see a person hell-bent on efficiency
To change society – no less – that is my claim
Thinking for you and representing your good name.

If ever you a politician see,
There stands a man hell-bent upon democracy
No place for master-servant, those who can't and can
My job if simply acting on behalf of everyman.

If ever you a politician see,
He'll try to tell you he's hell-bent on equality
The fact that some seem much more equal than the rest
Is not an argument with which I am impressed.

If ever you a politician see,
You won't expect him demonstrating too much modesty
If my claims are much too much, my leadership in doubt
Just take up politics – the only way to get me out!

If ever you a politician see,
You'll hear him arguing with, oh, such certainty
And by the time you challenge him and win
You'll be a politician too and just like him!

'THE LAWYER'

On my right the politician
On my left stands everyman
We know everybody's wishing
Each the other understand.

Stop a mess, avoid a bungle,
As we wade through all that law,
Treading through the legal jungle,
Expert guide is what I'm for!

Solicitor, advocate and barrister
Untying the legal knot,
Attorney, Judge and even Chancellor
Sorting out just what is what.

Tort and plaintiff, plea, defendant,
Tricky words I understand,
Ward-of-court and those dependant,
Lead you, layman, by the hand.

On my right the politician
On my left stands everyman,
In the middle my decision
To those who can't from those who can.

'INVENTOR'

If you're always doubting your own imagination
The Inventor has a mind which often leaps ahead,
With my creative brain and a little lateral thinking
"Don't fly on without me!" is the least that can be said.

If you have a problem – don't know how to tackle it,
Please don't be afraid to try to pick my brain.
When you find my answer – one you'd never thought of
Surely you will use my skills to help you out again.

Keeping a balloon buoyant in the atmosphere
Proves to be a problem quite well known to me
To solve it I use science and a modicum of genius
Which often saved people who were otherwise all at sea.

If you like the word 'if' or 'the merest possibility'
The chance of a solution is never far away,
Surrounding us everywhere the fruits of intuition
Finding such solutions is my effort day-by-day.

Inventors form a bridge from the present to the future
Man quickly takes for granted an inventor's skill,
Imagine a world which is never thinking forwards
Creating an inertia that's impossible to kill.

'DOCTOR'

I'm a doctor
I'm a doctor
I'm a necessary medical man
With my med'cines and pills
I can surely cure your ills

> Open wide – touch your toes – swallow hard – hold your nose
> - breathe out and breathe in – this will just prick your skin
> - see how that feels – every day, before meals –

There: I can help you find life's wealth
It's a simple thing called 'health'

You'd be very wise to save me if you can!

I'm a doctor
Yes, a doctor
I ensure the nation's health is of the best
Repairing bodies is my job
With my stethoscope and swab

> Slip them off – now say 'aaah' – can you really see that far? - let's just inspect your ears – the worst is over, it appears – it's no better, it's no worse – give your sample to the nurse – this should help to ease the pain – can you please come back again? - now please control those tears – he may live for several years.....

There: I can help in many ways
To extend your useful days

You'd be crazy to deny me to the rest
(Aren't you impressed?)
You'd be crazy to deny me to the rest!

'SOLDIER'

Airman – Sailor – Soldier
Uniformly dressed
Quite often we have told you
We represent the best.

In air and sea, across the land
Protecting everyone
'For Queen and Country' is our stand
We'll get them on the run.

'Them' is fairly complex
Who is it makes the fuss?
Anyone that we don't like
As long as it's not us.

When no-one really wants a war
Or when the battles cease
We have to face that awful bore
That dreadful thing called 'peace'!

'THE PHILOSOPHER'

What use is a philosopher
As the balloon slowly sinks?
On board we are in short supply
Of anyone who thinks!

I cannot cook an omelette
I cannot mend a tap
But like a thinking geographer
I draw the human map.

Terms and definitions
The use of logic too
The value of decisions
Is left to rather few.

Making sense of chaos
Sorting out the brain
Thinking much more clearly
I'm happy to explain.
(Well, I'll try to!)

'MOTHER-TO-BE'

Lodged inside my tummy
Is a horde of DNA
I'm soon to be a mummy:
I'm in the family way

My little, precious foetus
Is only mine to hold
Soon it will be here to greet us
The 'it' is 'him' I'm told.

His little toes and fingers
His pink and wrinkled face
Form the only future
For the human race.

Regrettably I'm heavy,
Weigh down this sad balloon,
But try to save the two of us
Who'll be here all too soon!

PROJECT

'Deepend'

This project concerns responsibility and the selfish versus the responsible aspects of ourselves.

The following cast can be chosen as the outline story unfolds, probably using volunteers.

The outline story: The piece starts at a local swimming club. The coach calls the swimmers out of the water and praises some of them for their hard work and improvement. One girl – Trudy – faces bad news and good news. She has been missing training sessions and is reprimanded. But it emerges that she is chosen for the national squad of advanced swimmers.

She tells her mother.

The scene moves to the country's training centre. Another coach meets the young talent. Settles them in their rooms; where they eat; time for the next morning's training at the poolside. They are also told to 'book out' if they leave the 'camp'.

Trudy meets a young swimmer who invites her to go into town. She joins him but doesn't book out.

A fire occurs in the hostel. The Fire Brigade come and try to put out the blaze. Checking the list the coach and Fire Chief can't account for Trudy. She must be in her room. A brave fireman agrees to try to rescue her. He goes in and is soon overcome by smoke and dies.

His widow is called and the firemen commiserate. As they do so the fireman's body is brought down. Trudy appears from town....

For the cast you will need:

>   Several swimmers
>   Their coach at the local club
>   Trudy
>   Trudy's mother
>   Coach at national level
>   The boy – a good swimmer
>   The Fire Chief and firemen
>   One (brave) fireman
>   His wife

>   (The local swimmers can become the national squad too)

This scene should be improvised, with due help from the teacher.

The swimmers will have to choose a stroke and even their training programme – what they must practise; and hard! This can include divers.

When they come out of the water they should dry themselves and put on their tracksuits as they listen to their local coach. When Trudy's selection is announced the group should applaud her generously.

Trudy tells her mother both bad and good news.

The national coach should be tough with them and promise only 'hard work'.

The young swimmer should be a champion and have some charm. Does Trudy forget to sign the book or just not bother?

Four firemen would be needed, including the Fire Chief. He links up with the coach. Find one 'brave' fireman. Perhaps he goes in with another who reports back that he is missing in the hostel.

Trudy appears – with a new boy friend. She faces the fireman's widow. And the body.

PROJECT

'Museum'
(Cross refer to the play of the same name)

Many museums have in recent years radically changed their practice from 'DO NOT TOUCH' to 'HANDS ON'. This, together with the 'Free entry to Museums' debate, has clearly provided access for thousands, especially of the young, who previously found these places to be forbidding and cold and expensive.

This project runs in the modern style, encouraging the experimental approach.

The group is free to design its own museum. The teacher creates groups of three or four. Each group has to choose a gallery in which some activity is both displayed but also demonstrated. Thus 'Shoe-making' shows how shoes were made. In the 'Papyrus' gallery the art of making paper is shown. Another may demonstrate 'Nappies through the Ages', etc. etc.

Time is given for groups to prepare. A deadline is announced for the opening of this new museum. Finishing touches are made and the Museum is ready to open its doors to the public.

But news comes from a higher source that there is a million pound shortfall in funding for this new venture. The director summons his staff in order to break this bad news. The staff must argue democratically on how to accept the cuts:

> Should entrance fees be brought in?
> Should perhaps three galleries be closed?
> Should everyone on the staff accept a pay cut?
> Should some valuable exhibit be put on the market for sale?
> Etc. etc.

Once decisions have been made the new museum makes the final preparations for receiving the public. Perhaps each 'gallery' has to be ready to receive a royal for the opening. Possibly print material even photography can be prepared and artefacts can be gathered, workshop materials, etc.

The general public attending the opening can be another class or group and they can be brought into a living 'hands-on' experience.

Some possible sections:

> Down the mine
> Life in Victorian England
> Colonizing Australia
> Splitting Siamese twins
> Polishing diamonds
> On the film set
> Training for the catwalk
> Making seaside rock
> Punch & Judy
> Dry stone walling, etc. etc.

Alongside this improvised 'museum' project is its counterpart, a texted play, printed in the earlier section.

PROJECT

'Finding a Job'

This is a play-making project in which the students create the drama from their own resources, simply fleshing out the following idea. This is an important part of the creative process whereby the student, even at a young age, can be author, director, actor – and, if need be – audience too.

The teacher should begin with a brain-storming session in which he/she asks the students to think of the 'kind of things' which feature in a job advertisement. Some actual adverts can be available cut out and mounted from local/national newspapers. Eventually the teacher (on the black/white board) can begin to list the categories of which the following is probably a full-enough list:

The name of the job
A brief description of the job
The qualifications/experience needed
The salary or wage offered
Something about the employer
Any special information, e.g. open to any age group, any ethnic group, etc.
How and where to apply.

Divide the full group into sub-groups of three each. They can give themselves a team name. Now, for about 20 minutes, invite them to compose a job advert – their own choice. By discussion. One of the three to be recorder or scribe. The teacher can circulate at this point, offering help on the need-to-know basis. The students firm up their advert, in readiness for Stage 2.

Let each of the trio name itself A, B and C. A becomes the interviewer, the employer, personnel officer. He sets up his interview space in a quiet part of the room. He/she works to the advert they have created and which the applicants also helped design. If working in mixed-ability groups perhaps the brightest student can be character A.

Once ready, character B comes into the room as candidate 1 and A interviews them, for the post advertised. Meanwhile all the Characters C are in some kind of waiting room. Here the teacher can join them and it adds spice to the project if the teacher comments to the (nervous) applicants. Thus: "Should you be wearing jeans for an interview like this?" "The person in with the boss at the moment looks very strong and experienced", "I hope you got a return rail ticket", or "You do look white, are you feeling OK?"

A's interview should last about five minutes. But A is non-committal. By the time C enters the interview room he should carry some level of trepidation even anxiety! A gives the second interview and the teacher can treat B as he did group C, earlier, in the waiting room.

The boss then has to make a judgement: B or C? In fact he may appoint neither. There are many strategies open to A. "I have decided to offer B the job but for a probationary period of three months". "I am going to offer you a shared appointment. B to work half time and C to work half time. What do you think?". "Are you willing to come unpaid for a trial period: to see if you like the work and we like you?" A can offer one of the pair a chance to interview him.

The project could end by B and C going to another A but they won't, of course, then know the job on offer. Each can have five minutes to read the job description. A good finish is for A, B and C to write to someone telling them what happened at The Interview: to their wife, mother, a colleague.

PROJECT

'Information Bureau'

'Information Bureau' is play-making. Based on the students' own ideas and improvisation it will take the shape of a short play but each effort will by definition be different from those that went before. It is difficult (but not impossible) to repeat any action. The spirit of it is improvisation and this involves risk-taking, spontaneity and strong imagination, as the following makes clear.

The central idea is that a town or city has developed a new idea for communicating to its visitors and clients. Instead of the normal maps, brochures, entertainment lists, this town can provide live, actuality to demonstrate its character, its facilities and strengths. Even its weaknesses!

Pivotal is a desk, manned by two staff. On one side of them are the clients who must think what it is they wish to know. On the other (as if hanging on coat-pegs) is a group of all-purpose actors instantly able to demonstrate aspects of life in the town. This group doesn't know what they have to do until they hear the clients' requests. Then they immediately spring into life. Clearly this requires both good organisation by the 'actors' but also some discretion by the clients. After all, the clients will rotate and become an 'actor' next time round so they had best only ask what is within the actors' scope. This give-and-take is central to improvisation work and, of course, to theatre itself. The following shows a useful layout for the space:

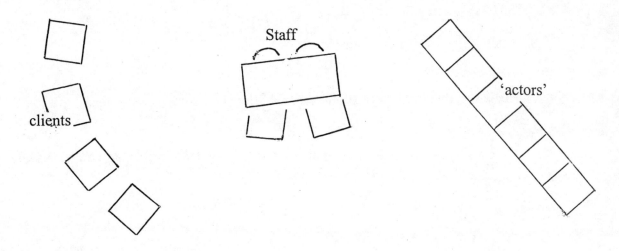

The staff can control the clients and can employ various techniques to give the 'actors' some breathing space. They can explain their new resource; they can offer it in slow-motion (or by using any film technique); they can offer it silent; they can repeat it, allowing the client to join in the activity.

It may help to run the exercise for a couple of times to allow the 'actors' to sort themselves out. For example on one occasion perhaps only two of the actors are needed and the rest can relax (on their coat-pegs!). One of the 'actors' could be responsible for leading in any movement or dance activity requested. This actor group could start with your eight more imaginative students. It will soon change, as client takes the place of one actor and that actor becomes a client.

To start the 'actors' demonstration it might be useful to have a simulated computer or simply a buzzer to begin the activity (and to end it).

The following list is merely a suggestion of the range of ideas that clients could request. Perhaps the two 'staff' could veto 'impossible' requests by a novice group while a more advanced group could try virtually anything thrown at them – even flight!

> "We're thinking of moving to this town and wish to bring my (aged) mother. What facilities have you for the elderly?"

> "My husband and I love Scottish dancing. Have you any groups we could join?"

> "We've heard that your town has some novel ideas for punishing those who drop litter. Could we know a little more?"

> "Is it possible to find out about your traditional wedding ceremonies?"

> "We've heard about the medieval practice of 'lug dangling'. Can you tell us any more?"

> "Could we visit a local school?"

"My family and I are animal-lovers. We gather you have some very rare species here?"

"Is it possible to visit a factory which makes seaside rock, and puts the town's name right through it?"

"Could we meet the original Father Christmas?"
Etc.

The clients must make their own requests and only use this list if they are stuck.

As has been said, as each client is satisfied with their 'answer' they leave and move in to take a place as an 'actor' while his actor joins the queue as a client.

After one or two trials the method becomes clear and the 'play' can develop. It is, of course, possible to run the activity in a second language or even a 'black' language.

Some more complex ideas:

"I'm a very lonely person, seeking friends. I have heard that everyone in this area is very welcoming and friendly, could you tell me any more?"

"I gather that Adolf Hitler planned his invasion of Europe in a little hotel here. Is that true?"

"Is this the town which has a well whose waters gives a person extra life and vitality?"

"My son wants to be a surgeon, could he watch an operation in your hospital?"

"You are in '*The Guinness Book of Records*' for making the world's biggest meat pie. Is it possible to know more about it?"

The spirit of improvisation strongly permits ideas like the above to be developed and any group could think up endless variations on the same theme and within this shape.

The efforts can be videotaped and edited into a 'best' programme; perhaps for future groups to see.

PROJECT

'The Surgery'

There is always a sense of authenticity and satisfaction when a drama project corresponds to the reality of the life it represents.

On this occasion – a doctor's surgery – life and drama can be very close. Of course the doctor-figure can hardly command the expertise of his real-life counterpart but essentially this doesn't matter. The various actors playing the medic can and will assume Dorothy Heathcote's 'mantle of the expert'. Even if the player is wildly wrong in his/her diagnosis and treatment we will have a comic scenario and can forgive this doctor for his/her inexperience or inefficiency. On the other side the patient is <u>us</u>. Few (and very lucky) people have no experience of being ill and attending a surgery. And there are few circumstances in life where the layman realises so much the value of professional help. Of course the client not the doctor is the person ill but a good doctor needs the patient's input to resolve the problem anyway.

The doctor-role rotates. In one 'room' we see this expert. A useful ploy is to have another actor 'sitting in' – as students/trainee doctors do.

In a larger space next door sit today's patients – this could occupy perhaps as many as 20 players. As in real life they can include a friend or relation who may be a patient or child, a neighbour, a driver.

A few minutes should be given to let the patient decide what their problem is. Perhaps they can choose a card which names a part of the body: ears, toes, back, knee; illness or injury. It could be a maternity clinic; or 'Weightwatchers'!

Pivotal to the scene should be the nurse, a part which can be taken by the teacher or a mature student. An older person, perhaps from a senior group, could well come in to take this role.

Before the clinic opens the teacher can explain that <u>either</u> the doctor's room can be heard <u>or</u> the waiting room. If the nurse is with the doctor the other group can speak and if the nurse is in the waiting room we can hear the doctor's consultation. This simple technique means that some order is maintained and everyone can hear what is happening.

Thus the nurse leads the first 'case' into the doctor's room and we hear the small-talk (if any) of the waiting group. Then the nurse goes through the door into the waiting room and we can hear the consultation. Of course 'action' can continue in the silent room.

As in real life the doctor has finite time in order to get through 'the list'. Perhaps 3 – 5 minutes should be allowed for each drama consultation. When the patient leaves they could go to a dispensary (in the practice) to get their prescription; even to visit a physio. This will need to be set up at the outset and may best be brought in 'second time round'.

Thus everyone is occupied and the nervous tension of the players can approximate the atmosphere found in many medical practices.

Here are some fragments of dialogue but no scripted text should be used, in the event. As in life, this is improvised and thrives on action/reaction.

A

Nurse:	What is your name, please?
Mrs L:	Ling, my name Mrs Ling.
Nurse:	I think I can spot your problem, Mrs Ling. It is in that cage there isn't it?
Mrs L:	That's right. Little Benny.
Nurse:	Little Benny. Who or what is Benny, Mrs Ling?
Mrs L:	Benny is a marmoset.
Nurse:	We don't like to disappoint – well, 'visitors' – but Dr Penakis is a doctor, not a vet, Mrs Ling.
Mrs L:	That doesn't matter nurse. Doctor really well qualified.
Nurse:	But in this country Mrs Ling doctors only look after humans.

Mrs L: Let me tell you Miss Nurse, Benny is part human, big part human. Benny has inherited the spirit of my late husband – also Benny. He dead but lived on in this Benny.

Nurse: Well I think the doctor will have to decide. Follow me -

(NB Here the nurse *is* allowed to speak)

B

Dr P: Do come in and sit down. Now (looking through papers) Mrs Ling, isn't it?

Mrs L: Yes, right.

Dr P: Where are you from Mrs Ling?

Mrs L: China. But not today, Soho today.

Dr P: I see. Now what seems to be the problem, eh?

Mrs L: Here. Inside is the problem, Benny.

Trainee Doc: It seems to be something like a squirrel, doctor.

Mrs L: No squirrel. Marmoset. Benny is marmoset.

Dr P: I see. Now Mrs Ling – do you understand me. I'm a doctor Mrs Ling. Veronica show her my certificates. Now doctors Mrs Ling just don't do marmosets. That's veterinary surgeons.

Mrs L: But Benny bit me, doctor. Here (specifies). He bit hand. Sharp teeth. Just like my husband.

Dr P: Sorry, I don't understand.

Mrs L: My late husband also Benny. When he die part of his spirit live in this Benny. Then Benny bite.

Dr P: Which Benny bit you Mrs Ling? Veronica, could you take over. I feel I need a little break---

As was mentioned, the doctor-character can rotate. Perhaps each time round a doctor could see three clients before becoming one himself. The latest patient can step into the doctor's role – simply by donning a white coat and the traditional stethoscope. The doctor becomes another patient.

Dr: Do come in and sit down. Now Fred Smith isn't it? We haven't met for six years. Now, tell me the problem, Fred.

Fred: It's my wrist, doctor. I seem to have a pain in it all the time now. And it's been getting worse.

Dr: Let me see (he takes the wrist and flexes and rotates it). Did that hurt?

Fred: Mmm!

Dr: What's your work Fred?

Fred: I work in the flooring trade – vinyl and carpets. That kind of thing.

Dr: Well you've almost certainly got what we call RSS – Repetitive Strain Syndrome. It's an overstrain on the muscles and damage in that area. You are right-handed Fred, aren't you?

Etc....

Doctor's   Waiting

'A SHORT APPRAISAL OF SHORT PLAYS'

The one-act play form and its place in drama has been the subject of considerable speculation. If we relate the concept to the novel we find that the short story is seen as a specialised creative act and one to which the greatest writers brought their skills. Of course the novel which forms a direct line between writer and reader in either its full or shorter form makes its impact direct into a single imagination. The short form may suit the needs of the reader with limited time or stamina. Many of the greatest writers tried their hand at the short story and the best of these are masterpieces per se. Some writers chose only to work in the short form.

In the theatre the short play – or so-called one act play – requires a collective audience to enter into the 'willing suspension of disbelief' as with the full-length play. But this audience is in itself a problem. For three hundred or three thousand people to turn out and turn up for a single 40 minute play is not viable in either artistic or economic terms. The whole process of attending theatre Shakespeare described well as "the two hour traffic of the stage". As these days one might well be two hours **in** traffic reaching the theatre anything less would seem to short-change the audience! Very rarely has a single short play been staged and the usual practice in this respect has been to form a double bill, possibly on a related theme; possibly a contrasting pair; sometimes with a mutual cast.

But, of course, this is not so with television drama where the prevailing drama in the soap operas specialises in the short form; the half hour episode which forms a link between two episodes and demands the audience's attention. Here the characters and often the plot are continuous and the viewer probably starts with a detailed knowledge of the setting, the characters and probably the situation being resolved. In the theatre the cast has to begin from scratch and the generally-held view is that 30 to 40 minutes is simply too short a time to develop more than a superficial view of either character or plot. The focus here had best sharpen itself on to one or two characters and on to any event which can be established, developed, resolved in the short space of time allowed. In this respect there is scant time for a sub-plot to emerge. In the lengthier 'King Lear' the Gloucester sub-plot throws light onto the tragic failure of the King. Here Gloucester's blindness echoes Lear's moral blindness as the two plots inform and deepen each other. No such luxury is available to the writer of the one act, short play.

In fact several writers now considered 'major' have tried the short play. Checkov, Anouilh and more recently Pinter and Shaffer have turned their hands to the unitary play. This may have been as a test piece for a young playwright and/or a hope in modern times to have the piece slotted in to television schedules. It may be because the writer wished to focus on a single issue and explore it fully. Thus 'Black Comedy' explored the idea of reversing light and dark and within that idea many comic points can emerge. In Harold Pinter's early work one feels he is doing for his trade what Leonardo da Vinci did in his wonderful sketches which remain brilliant in their own right. Anouilh's 'Antigone' remains one of the best short plays but at one and a half hours length it can stand alone. In fact it is essentially a debate between Creon and Antigone. The writer believes that 'A Phoenix too Frequent' by Christopher Fry is the very best of the short-play form. Simpson, Ionesco and Becket restricted their absurd efforts to one act and some would attest that this genre may be impossible to sustain for longer.

In writing various 'plays' for young people one is aware of the shortcomings of character and situation which one faces. Fifteen minute 'sketches' (American 'skits' – for that may be the word) – can hardly develop much in depth – character or plot. And with larger casts the opportunities are even less for the establishment of character. But such pieces can validly illustrate small situations and even problems – perhaps enough to engage younger players. In such cases the sketch contains some essential problem or tension, however simplified, with which the characters struggle. Such pieces often leave the issue unresolved whereas the dramatist with his two hours can often point to solutions to problems and take the audience to depths unavailable in a few minutes. Sometimes one fears that a fifteen minute piece may be the extent of a young audience's concentration in the present climate!

The actors in such short sketches have to work very hard to establish their credibility, their 'life', in a few exchanges. What would be exposition in a full-length play becomes the play itself. Clearly such short pieces are prone to make for two-dimensional characters and even stereotypes as those depicted are in 'shorthand'. But the sketch has its place and should only whet the appetite for longer stuff.

The sketch will certainly permit simple staging and then invoke more from the audience's imagination. As these present sketches are for young (including second-language) learners and for strictly limited time scales (eg a lesson) they have a distinct place – an étude as opposed to a full concerto! They are easily learnt and would not require a prolonged rehearsal period.